. . . all I ever wanted to do was paint light on the walls of life.

Lawrence Ferlinghetti
"More Light"

Light on the Walls of Life

Light on the Walls of Life

a tribute anthology to
Lawrence Ferlinghetti

edited by Bobby Coleman

Jambu Press
an expression of

Studio Saraswati
www.jambupress.com
San Francisco

Jambu Press
an expression of Studio Saraswati
www.jambupress.com / www.studiosaraswati.com
saraswati.sf@gmail.com
San Francisco, California

Printed in the United States of America with eco-certified materials
First Edition, First Printing

Book concept and design by Virginia Barrett
Back cover photo of Ferlinghetti by Dominic Angerame, 2003
Text set in Baskerville, titles in DIN Alternate
Images without attribution are credited to the Jambu Press team

Produced in the unceded ancestral homeland of the Ramaytush Ohlone
peoples, the original inhabitants of the San Francisco Peninsula

Honoring Lawrence Ferlinghetti's wishes for this tribute anthology, proceeds
from book sales benefit educational public programs in poetry and arts
literacy; please visit www.jambupress.com for more information

Library of Congress Control Number: 2020951534
ISBN-13: 9781734146011
Jambu Press is a member of CLMP

for Lawrence Ferlinghetti
(1919–2021)

Of your own sweet Self still sing
yet utter 'the word en-masse'—

"Populist Manifesto No. 1"—Ferlinghetti

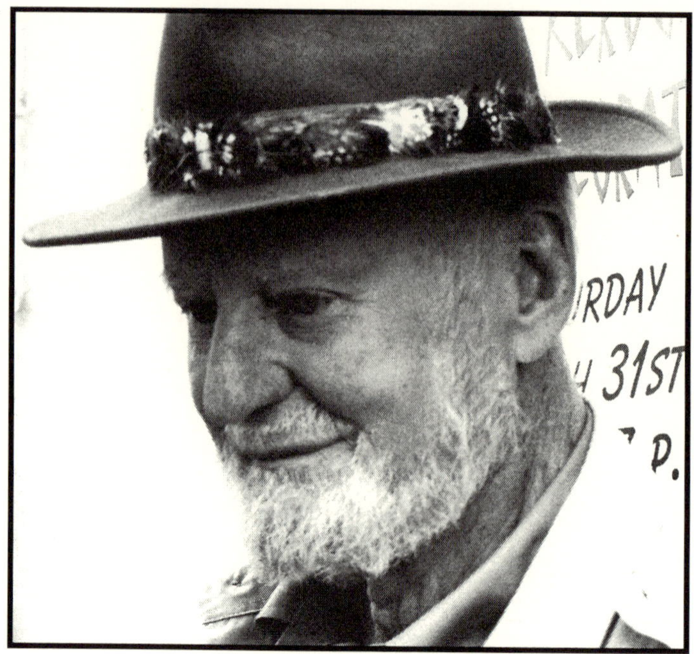

Ferlinghetti at a public celebration of City Lights' 50th Anniversary, 2003
Dominic Angerame

Throughout this collection, most lines in italics within poems are by Lawrence Ferlinghetti. Given the *own sweet Self* styles of poets, however, not all borrowed lines are italicized and not all italicized words/lines are borrowed. Centos (collage poems) consisting entirely of Ferlinghetti lines are not in italics (pp. 35, 48). Please consult the Notes section (pp. 178–9) for additional attributions and the sources of other quoted lines.

The brief references and short phrases quoted in this homage to Ferlinghetti will surely prompt an appetite for his writings. An extensive bibliography can be found on City Lights Booksellers & Publishers' website, citylights.com. His books are published by New Directions, City Lights, Liveright/W. W. Norton, Doubleday/Penguin Random House, Sore Dove Press, and others around the world.

Contents

1 - Riffs

2 - Tidings

3 - Happy 100th, Lawrence!

4 - Tales

5 - In Memoriam

List of Images

Unattributed images throughout the book are by the Jambu Press team. Images with lines by Ferlinghetti include the title of the poem from which they originate (pp. 11, 15, 22, 45, 93, 103, and 118), except p. 137 with lines from "Matinal."

Editor's Note

Bobby Coleman

Dear Reader,

Lawrence Ferlinghetti (1919–2021) was a poet, writer, publisher, painter, co-founder of City Lights, social activist, and arts catalyst, all with simultaneous excellence. In addition to poetry, he wrote fiction, translation, plays, art criticism, film narration, and essays. This tribute volume was authorized by Ferlinghetti shortly before his 100th birthday. He had contributed poems to two of the publisher's earlier anthologies and expressed his hope that this book would likewise support the advance of poetry and general artistic literacy. Honoring his wishes, proceeds from the book's sales will benefit community educational programs toward that goal.

In these pages, 74 talented contributors—renowned writers and visual artists as well as impressive newer voices—together respond to Ferlinghetti's example, similarly demonstrating the lasting sacred power of poetry and insurgent art. They are strongly encouraging us, with great passion, to also be inspired.

Ferlinghetti resisted conformity with steady confidence. Despite using unconventional and challenging sources for his glimpses of universal and personal transcendence, this robustly non-pandering, optimistically spiritual, yet blatantly tough social observer succeeded in getting over a million copies of one of his books of poetry, *A Coney Island of the Mind,* into people's hands and hearts. Though he gained wide celebrity, he generously avoided traditional notions of fame and identity. His standards were adamantly high. He could be compellingly sweet and appropriately forceful at the same time, consistently maintaining a very strong curiosity paired with a healthy and practical philosophy of justice.

He was warm and welcoming, both as a deeply-held personal value and as a countercultural statement, and he remains hugely beloved in return. His "temple" to the literary arts, City Lights Booksellers and Publishers, is equally treasured and loved. City Lights thrives impressively, continuing its magnificent service to literature and culture while staying committed to positive social ethics. Its whole staff is in perpetual bloom. City Lights turns 70 in 2023.

The title of this book is taken from Ferlinghetti's essay "More Light," in which he describes his motivation. It's not a simple metaphor, of course, as he often made clear. It also matches the way his eyes shimmered and reflected light in a very rare way, as though life itself found special brilliance in an inclusive, humanistic vision.

One may still fairly ask, how could such an anti-Establishment, West Coast-transplanted, Italo-Sephardic, independently Catholic, Buddhist-influenced, Jewish Ladino poet garner all that popular support? Is it his untethered, socially-conscious multicultural pacifism? Is it his San Francisco funhouse style, a free-spirited Whitmanesque romp, a collectively-principled narrative on a musically rhythmic rollercoaster ride? Is it his poetry of word-painting, nature, laughter, and eternal beauty? All of these elements come alive in this book. Each contributing poet and artist, in connecting with Ferlinghetti's viewpoint, artistically elopes with it. You're holding in your hands much more than a tribute. There's a sense of projecting these core values into a future where they'll shine and prevail. There are some of the same feelings of optimism one might experience at a wedding party or a ceremony for a newborn baby. From this basis, love is expressed on every page.

Lawrence Ferlinghetti's impressive light, we ardently hope, is here reflected again as it was in his eyes, spurred by the luminosity of his original works. For readers beginning or continuing their explorations of Ferlinghetti and of poetry, or of art as a creative transformational force, the massive enthusiasm in this collection will open many fruitful doors and windows. And playfully, with joy!

On his 100th birthday Ferlinghetti heard a choir singing to him as a surprise under his window. He started waving his scarf at them in appreciation, a bit like a boy playing musical conductor. So, let's play along with Ferlinghetti and the contributors in this book. Let's together stay playful, curious, full of wonder, and full of light.

Light on the Walls of Life

a tribute anthology to

Lawrence Ferlinghetti

1

Riffs

each verb a stallion
reared up against all ignorance
Untamed rampant radicals
in dictionaries of light

"Dictionaries of Light"—Ferlinghetti

serious Funky Bay dog

Juan Felipe Herrera

after "Dog"—Ferlinghetti

swaggin'

down Columbus
cross Broadway serious Funky Bay dog
ahead of me swaggin' thru Covid news
Republican showdown delirium beat
pass the ol' Tattoo Rose Café
pass the ol' bait shop & the last joint where
Oscar Z. Acosta was last seen no one knows
got a Buddhist chant
cookin' in my blood
Om Mani Padme HUM baby
video of the Lama poppin' thru my pods

what happened to the dude in the box
Aquatic Park slappin' congas below

what happened to your
painted Aquarius signs tell me
my fortune carnal but you are not here
slashing bead strings for 3 bolas
serious
astral
serious Funky Bay dog leans to the left
like all dogs seeking liberation from the trash life

we hobble & notice Muni pier
curves into the big Nothing galaxy sugar
somewhere beyond this Blue Dot
Earth world maybe reddish-orange Mars
interplanetary sprinkles past lives
step to gabardine grasp
illusions gone sisters gone brothers
ice shrapnel hulas of Saturn
the civilization cartographies

of Henry Louis Morgan were wrong by 99.99 degrees
you were wrong Henry

there were no savages
there were no barbarians
there was no civilization

serious Funky Bay dog all we have are these dresses
we're wearing tossed & charred crab shells
dog fish gut you go i go you go i go
astral dancin' on the green piers
Costanoan & Miwok hills
turquoise kodachrome i float with Chagall

slo-mo down below the villages &
red horses half erased the Vastness riddles in
Funky Bay dog cries freedom Funky Bay dog cries
all the violence all the violence
all the shopping carts all the wireless ten thousand
tons of hydrogen fuel for the solar orb per second
ten million sufferings
across each ranch to each town to each city
we
stroll
down
Columbus Avenue & Ginsberg's journals
Indian journeys inside the jelly heart caves
Ferlinghetti now the waters the Coney Island comes
blue-black prophecies & arousals homelands
salt & humanity
salt & humanity & bread
silver bracelets of trans lovers the Wharf
& the Laughing Woman from Playland
stuffed in the penny museum by the Bay Tours
come out come out yes come out

i stroll to Molinari's going Nowhere

my metaphysical needs gone now

my performative flags of time culture & power
history & Peter Max brush against my face
jimi hendrix at Winterland
Huey Newton fundraiser by the yellow-green park
gone now gone now you hear me

America Archipelago
                    Archipelago
                                        America

torn shredded blasted cut-off i am here
for the blessing alone with my Funky Bay dog
alone with the Aloners & their lone dogs
for the healing the totality
the clear mind shoveling the clear blaze

serious Funky Bay dog ambles ahead
rushes a one-leg crow
feed that tiny saint some Thai food from the green papaya truck
keep on rockin' the field
pinkish mansions to my left let it go brother sister
Ahimsa
Karuna the Lama says that's right Funky Bay dog

what happened to magic

for Lawrence

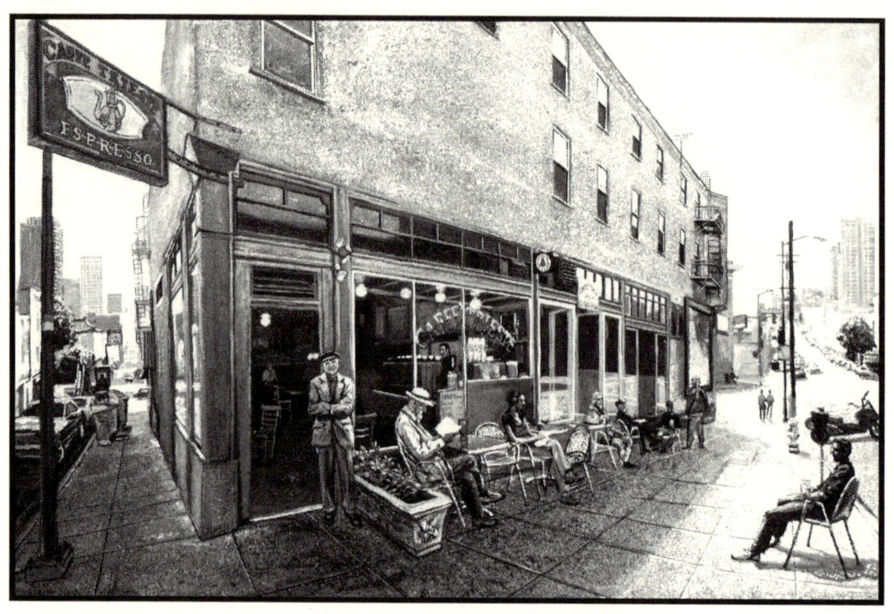

The Trieste **Anthony Holdsworth**
24" x 35" oil on canvas, 2010

The Caffe Trieste is one of my favorite subjects to paint in North Beach. On this occasion I had the good fortune to have both Papa Gianni and Lawrence Ferlinghetti pose for me onsite. —A.H.

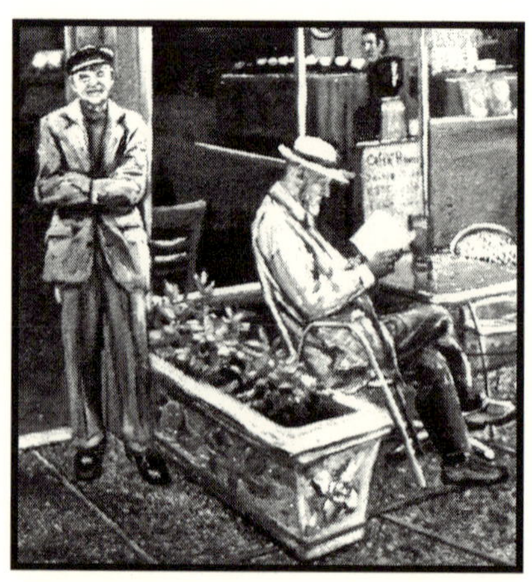

North Beach Meander

Frank Donnola

> And then the veil of light of early evening
> And then another scrim
> when the new night fog
> floats in
>
> "The Changing Light"—Ferlinghetti

Laundry dries pinned to the rail
of the second story fire escape,
next to some kid's graffiti sideways down.
That brick wall looks into the poets' room,
upstairs at City Lights,
where an old rocking chair has got me.
But really it's the words, the wondrous words have me now.
Rising above traffic noise, Chinese radio music
sifts through the window's metal grill.
Icy air confirms February's presence,
while the sun burns a hole in the haze.
Back on Columbus Avenue, streets
come at you from all angles;
a cautious casual whiplash guides you safely on.
Along narrow sidewalks, crowded with cafe tables,
a swift, shifting jerky shuffle is best.
Too many Italian restaurants call out like Sirens.
Espresso, the neighborhood house wine,
waits on each corner to jump-start your brain.
The actual beach, long since buried, was under
Francisco Street, where Italian fishing boats once rested.
Twelve Chinese women dancercize
around Washington Square, the Tao
of Busby Berkeley, it appears.
Looming over the park—Saints Peter & Paul church,
Dover's white cliffs carved by Michelangelo.
A man, a bull, an eagle, a lion—all with wings—
preside over the first line of Dante's *Paradiso*,
announcing how the glory of the Prime Mover
penetrates shining through the universe.
Air's transparency fools you into forgetting

how all manner of wavelengths crash against you;
your so-called spider-sense clutters up with static.
Damned if I didn't forget again my aluminum foil hat.
Somehow here in North Beach, though,
the jangling frequencies subside, the microwaves recede.
Their void is happily filled—with poetry, vino and pasta,
with Carol Doda's fabled go-go dance, and the ghosts
of old Beatniks rubbing shoulders in the fog.

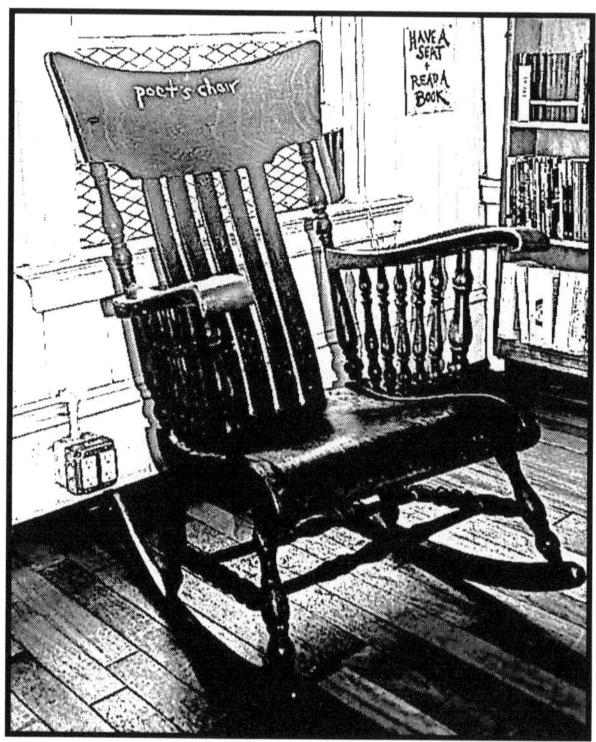

Poetry Room I

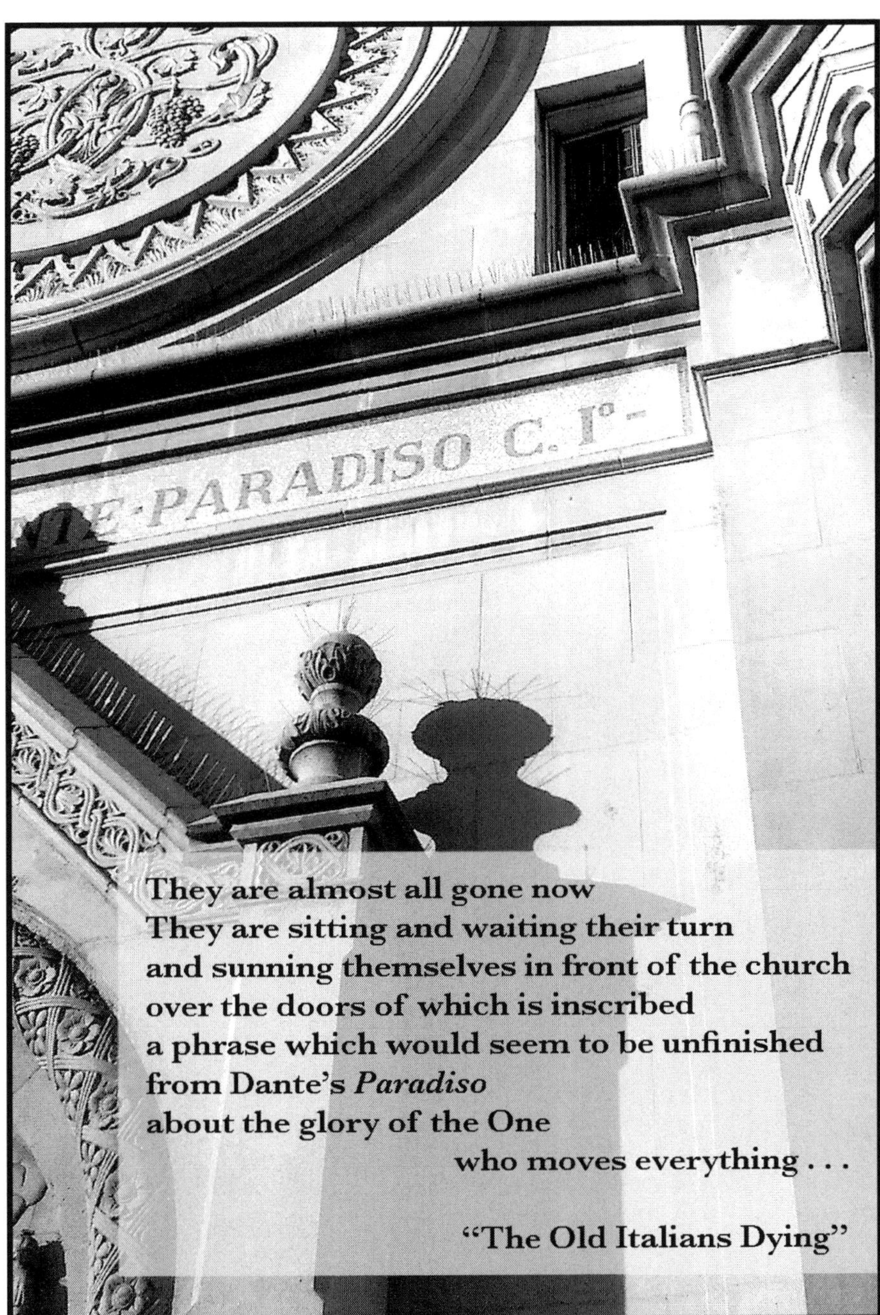

They are almost all gone now
They are sitting and waiting their turn
and sunning themselves in front of the church
over the doors of which is inscribed
a phrase which would seem to be unfinished
from Dante's *Paradiso*
about the glory of the One
who moves everything . . .

"The Old Italians Dying"

Away above a harborful
of caulkless houses
among the charley noble chimneypots
of a rooftop rigged with clotheslines
"Away Above a Harborful"—Ferlinghetti

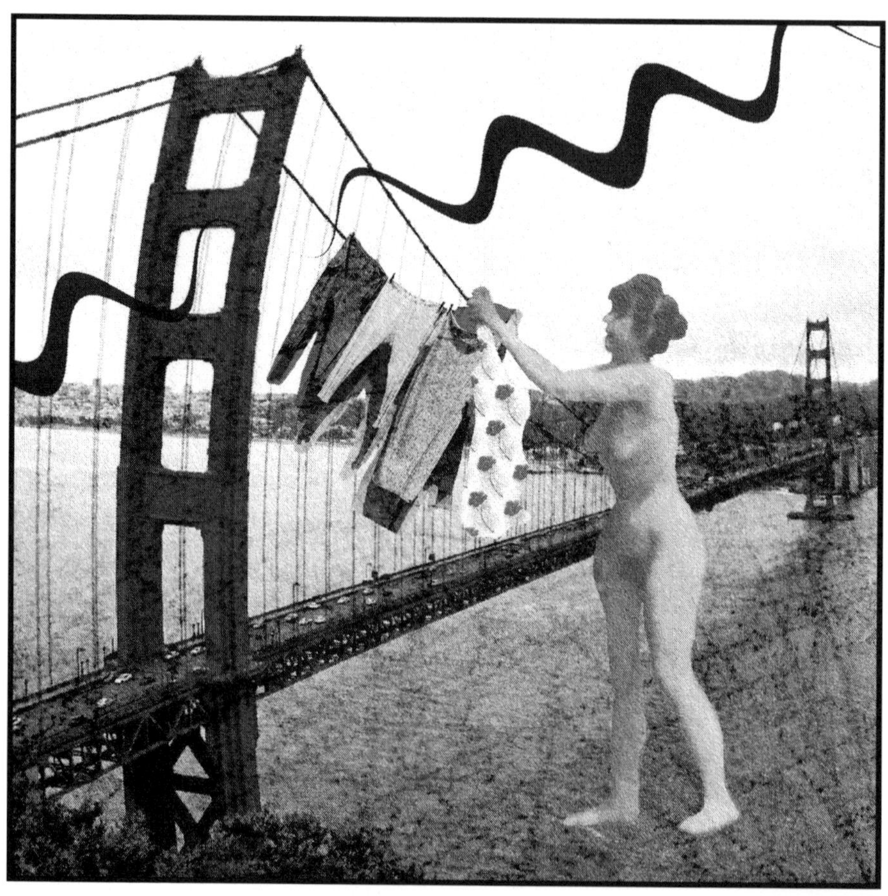

Oh lovely mammal **Ashley Pryor Geiger**
digital collage, 2020

Aquatic Park

Jessica Loos

> An old salt
> sits staring out
> at the sea
> "At Sea"—Ferlinghetti

The deceived sea, full of fish, seaweed
its salt fizzes in sand
then waves recede back
into the rest of water
taking things

The Marin hills, hazy, gray today,
bored in the white fog light
holding up the bridge

A fishing boat motors by,
headed for the Farallon
to drop pots for crab

A seal butterflies past the SS Jeremiah,
as the sun drowns in the tide,
closing in on shifting water

Editor's note: like Ferlinghetti, the SS *Jeremiah O'Brien* was in naval service during D-Day in Normandy and then in the Pacific. Now a "Liberty ship" museum, she is peacefully berthed on the San Francisco waterfront a short walk from where Ferlinghetti lived. One of the last of her kind, she is still seaworthy.

Anchorless in the Light

Andrena Zawinski

And in that veil of light
the city drifts
anchorless upon the ocean
"The Changing Light"—Ferlinghetti

It starts this way each morning—house wrens
flirting potato vines, spray of sea on sand,
then the crows and their warnings, mornings
dewy under sun. Come step onto the porch with me,

the view no longer blocked by the diseased pine.
We have this the gift of water beyond the marina,
its rocky channel gateway to a smooth bay.
Listen with me to buoys singing with wind in the fog,

old tug announcing its entry against the bark of a seal,
swoop of pelican wings. I cannot resist lingering here
in this veil of white light blinding with beauty, reminding
to hold onto this, hold it close and dear.

I was once stuck inside glass and brick, sight set
on neighboring city decks, their chatter, drunken songs
and brawls, all of it weedy with ivy, bats circling chimneys,
unlike these distant hills yet to be peopled. But last night

I dreamed their mounds became an unlit stretch of halls,
splintered doors on every wall, dust motes flecking air
over a muddy cliff where nothing stirred, except a ghastly
parade of dead who nodded, waved, winked, then dissipated,

sending my heart pounding. Here in this new day I can moor,
watch with steadied breath the rise of light. Come here.
I want you at my side, want you to look and listen with me
to the mourning dove's coo, anchorless in the light.

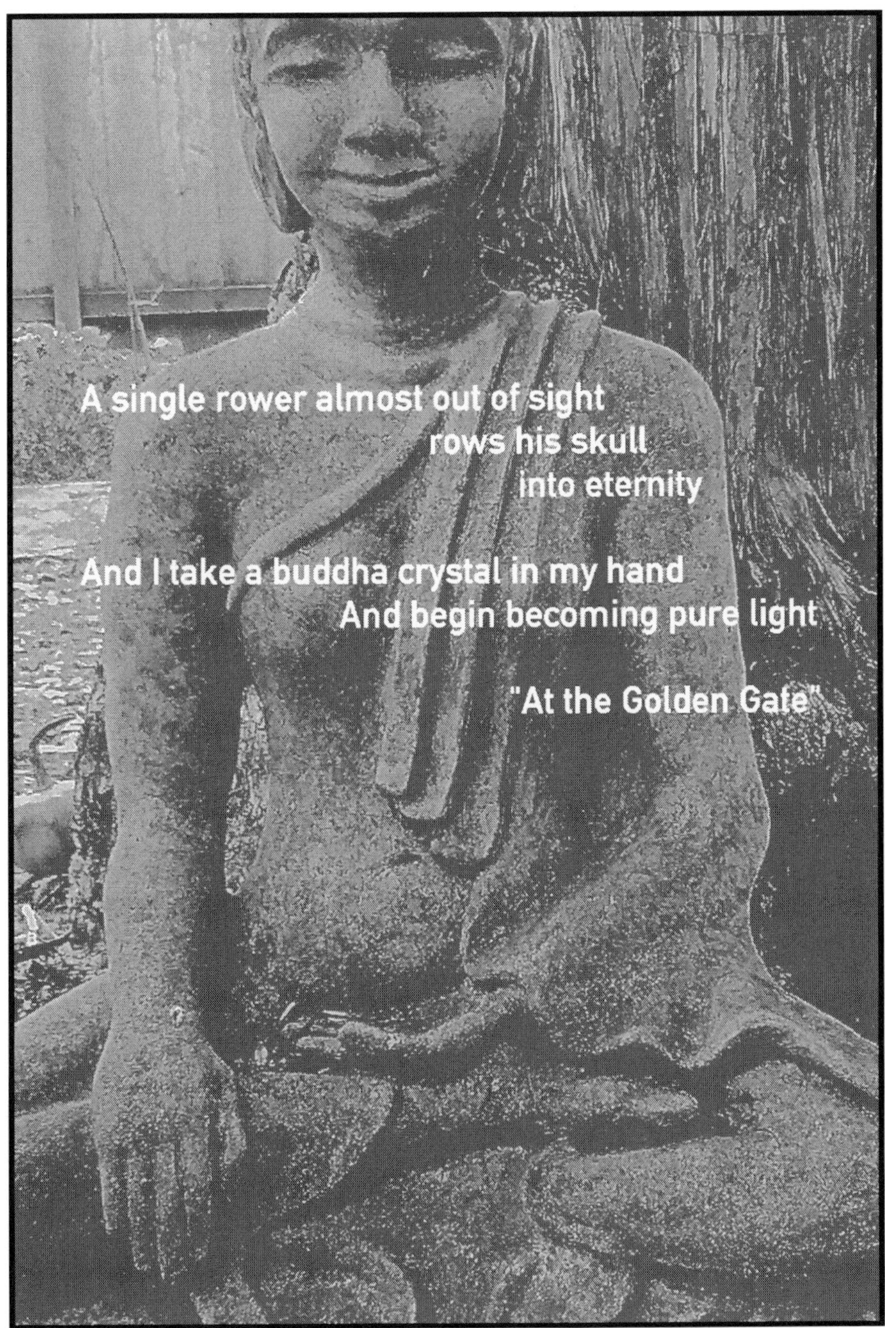
A single rower almost out of sight
rows his skull
into eternity
And I take a buddha crystal in my hand
And begin becoming pure light
"At the Golden Gate"

Poets from the Cold, Sacred Grounds in the Light

Clara Hsu

All that is lost must be looked for once more.
"Moscow in the Wilderness, Segovia in the Snow"—Ferlinghetti

Wednesday night in the city
magic still rules.
Ink-soaked papers
creased inside shirt pockets, pant pockets
coat pockets and pocket books have mouths,
mouths that articulate sounds from native soil to distant lands,
mouths that ride on bikes and in cars.
The #21 Hayes bus driver
sees El Duende, white hair and beard,
dances his way into the Sacred Grounds,
kisses the old Druidess and her flowing hair
as the Wounded God hollers, "Hear ye, hear ye!"
to the first unfolding of words.

Ghosts now, they still occupy their seats.
For over forty years the dark green divan
holds the weight of poets coming in from the cold.
They warm their bodies next to each other
laughing, singing, cursing, bickering
mulling under the wood-paneled ceiling and bright globe-lamps
staring at Marilyn Monroe and the second-hand arts
writing furious versions.

Sentinels of the sacred space—
the lesbians, the Sudanese, the Caucasian, the Chinese—
sweep away crumbs, mop up spills
keep the coffee hot and lights burning.
Burning
for the Buddha of the Bayou
for Matchless Goddess
for the Bard of the Lower Haight
for Coyote and its two-legged nemesis
for Emerson, Shakespeare

Edgar and his Nevermore
for Emily, H.D., Sylvia and Anne
they keep the lights burning
for the harmonica and saxophone jazz
for the out-of-tune guitar and its tremulous songstress
they keep the lights burning
on this sacred evening
in this sacred fog city
this Sacred Grounds Cafe
at this sacred hour
they keep the lights burning

for the beast, the angel and the madman.

Editor's note: the San Francisco Bay Area's inclusive tradition of oral poetry has spanned several generations. Ferlinghetti was a lead participant. Sacred Grounds Open Mic Poetry series in San Francisco has convened every Wednesday evening at 7 p.m. since 1972. It proclaims itself "the longest-running open mic poetry venue we know of" and it does appear to be the longest unbroken series of its type. Clara Hsu started attending in 2001. Poet-Druidess Jehanah Wedgewood presided for 19 years. Poet Dan Brady has been the intrepid host since December 2010.

Playland of the Mind

César Love

Perhaps there are shores of Heaven
Where deceased amusement parks go
Playland at the Beach would be there

A few of its novelties are still with us
Laffing Sal at Fisherman's Wharf
Camera Obscura at the Cliff House
The Fun House is now black and white
A cameo in an Orson Welles movie
There at the end of *The Lady from Shanghai.*

Playland is a memory to many
But condos and a Safeway to more.

My own memory is a camera without film.
Was I ever there?
I would have been very young
I have a blurry picture
of a cloudy white day
At a happy place near the ocean.
In sharper focus, yet just beyond the frame:
A merry-go-round in waltz,
The roller coaster set to pounce,
And ageless Laffing Sal.

Was I ever at Playland?
I could ask my mother
But any answer would ruin the spell.
It would be like asking,
Was my father really friends with William Burroughs?

Ocean winds shoulder their way across the Great Highway
A cascade of shrieks echoes from the roller coaster dive

I have never been to Coney Island

But I have been to Playland at the Beach
And my father was friends with William Burroughs.

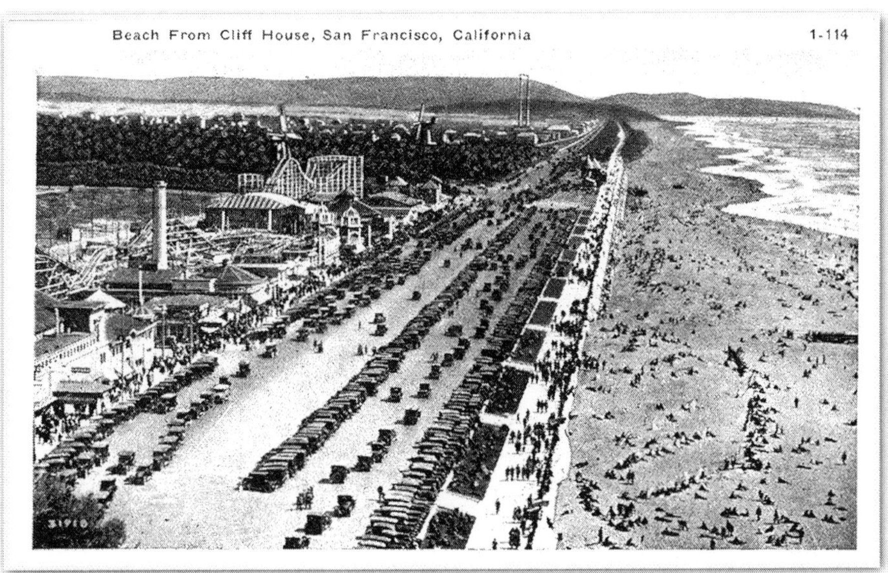

Illustrated postcard from the mid-1920s showing San Francisco's Playland at the Beach, Golden Gate Park, the Dutch and Murphy Windmills, a newly-constructed portion of the Great Highway and Esplanade, the original Beach Chalet (right of the highway), and Ocean Beach.

now over ocean
now over land
high over pinwheels stuck in sand
where a rollercoaster used to stand
"Seascape with Sun & Eagle"—Ferlinghetti

Normal Forest

Kenneth Pobo

> I am leading a quiet life
> outside of Mike's Place every day
> watching the world walk by
> in its curious shoes.
>
> "Autobiography"—Ferlinghetti

I have a forest inside me.
Birds fill the trees.
Bears kill living things.
My friend Delia says she has
this same forest only her trees
grow purple. Mine stay green,
so very normal. Sometimes
I sit beside a lonely fern
and listen to the moon's white
basketball falling through
a leaf hoop. The game ends
by morning.

I meet my grandmother here
when she's needing a break
from heaven, a normal place
with normal gold streets
that no one walks on—
they're hard on your spiritual feet.
She likes the forest hush.
I do too. We don't need to talk.
Put two clouds together—
they speak for both of us.

Home

Adrian Arias

> Poetry is a high house echoing
> with all the voices
> that ever said anything crazy or wonderful
> *What is Poetry?*—Ferlinghetti

In the dark I wonder
What is house?

Sometimes I feel that the only house I have is my body
until the body abandons me
and again I am not knowing what is happening with me.

If poetry is the only mystery
that clarifies the soul
poetry can be my house
until she finds out that I live there
without paying rent.

Homeless around the world
I do not care to know where or when
I just want you to read the word
CASA
written on my body
when they see me tremble at night.

House is root and it is cloud
sometimes it does not let you leave your origins and sometimes
you fly so high that you forget
the origins.

House is the easiest concept to understand
for those who do not have one
and it is the most difficult to understand
when you have a bed to sleep in every night.

I take my house everywhere
it's the easiest thing to transport that I own

and occupies only the space that I occupy
with my ideas and my feelings.

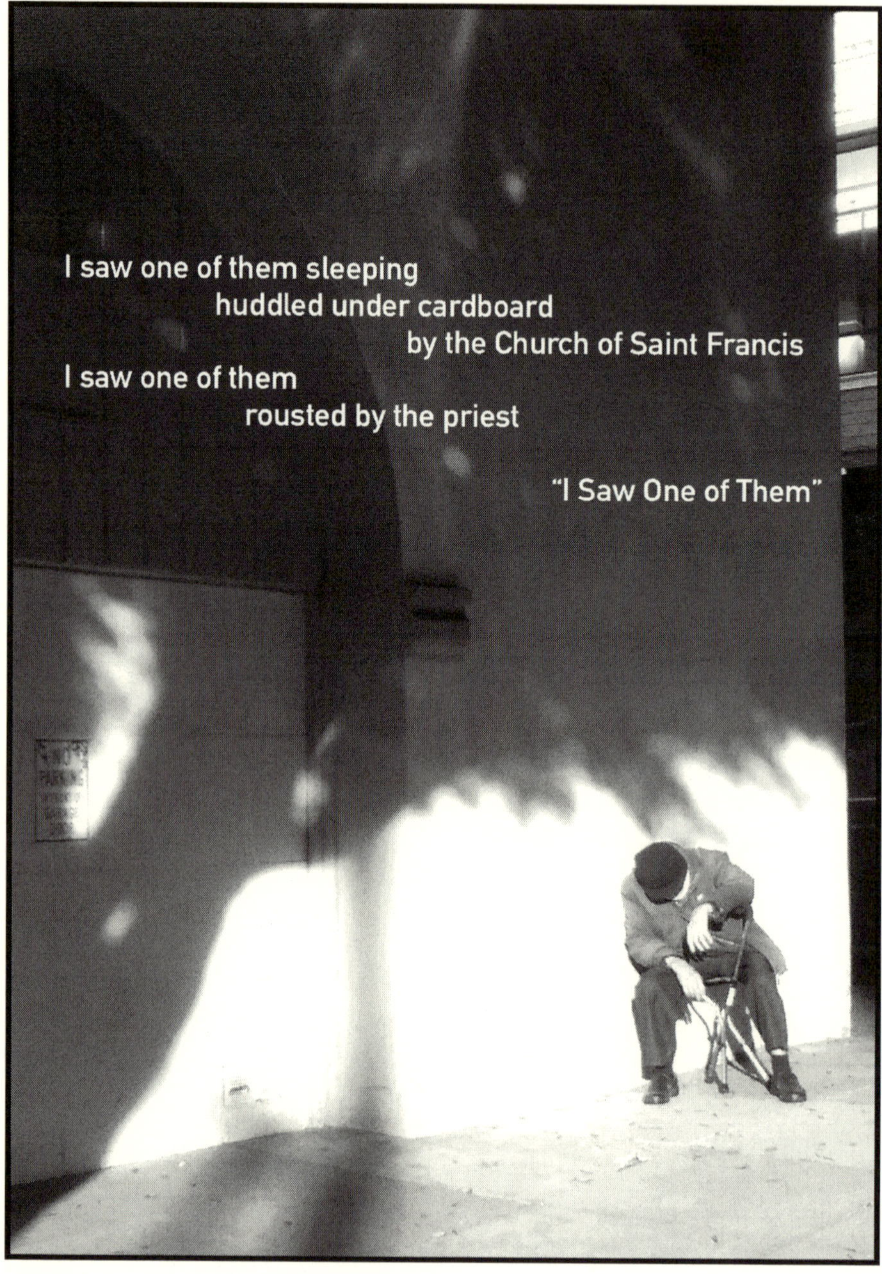

For Iris Canada

Tommi Avicolli Mecca

she just wanted to go home
just wanted to sit
on the red couch in the living room
watch her favorite programs
the dozens of photos
on the table and the walls
the paintings her
dead husband did
half a century of memories
in that old apartment
in the Fillmore
the sound of the jazz clubs
the laughter of the people
she used to know
were always with her as
she lay in the hospital
her heart racing
it wouldn't stop racing
the court condemned her
though she wasn't guilty
sheriff changed the locks
so the owners could
condo convert
make more money
she took sick after they
evicted her
moved her things
while she was in intensive care
everything she owned
all the photos
the paintings
they couldn't erase the memories
didn't matter that she was
100 years old
didn't matter that she
was one of the last Black people

on her block
in a city whose Black population
is down to five percent
didn't matter that
she died just wanting
to go home

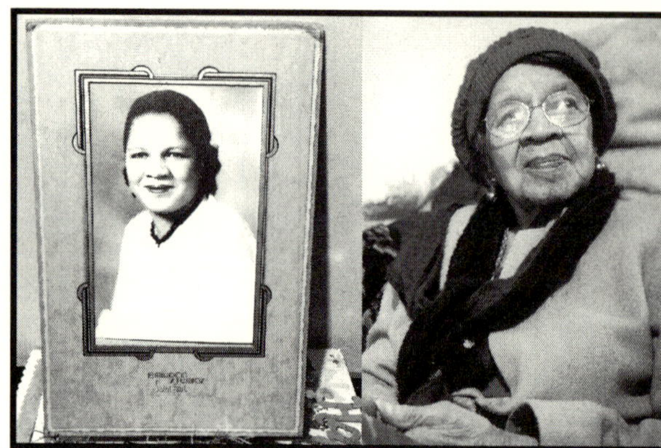

We are San Francisco, we are supposed to be compassionate and humane, but this is what we did to a senior in our city.
—Tommi Avicolli Mecca, *48 Hills*, March 27, 2017

photo / Housing Rights Committee of San Francisco

Editor's note: in response to our call for submissions, we received "For Iris Canada" soon after Ferlinghetti turned 100. His solidarity with this fellow centenarian was easy to imagine.

Two Women with Bags

Virginia Barrett

as if anything at all were possible
between them
across that small gulf
in the high seas
of this democracy
"Two Scavengers in a Truck, Two Beautiful People
in a Mercedes"—Ferlinghetti

At 27th two women disembark from the streetcar
and cross Church. One is casually
coifed, early forties—brunette hair pulled
back; she wears slacks and a dark
blazer in the style of a classic
Bostonian. Straight-
backed and balanced, she carries
in each hand
a rectangular shopping bag with handles made
from delicate cord: silver and white
Anne Taylor, Tiffany blue. The bags swing
slightly beside her like bowing
attendants as she strides to
Duncan, unsmiling.

The second woman wears a startling
grin, gray hair chopped bluntly
to her ears, she moves
close to the ground, a squat
Asian elder far from the province
of her girlhood. She balances
a long wooden pole across her shoulders, one arm looped
over it, plastic bags
dangling from either end, stuffed fat
with discarded
bottles and cans. She beelines
toward a receptacle
near me—the bags bobbing
like small bloated
bodies in the sea.

from I Am Also Waiting

Joanie HF Zosike

> I am waiting
> perpetually and forever
> a renaissance of wonder
> "I Am Waiting"—Ferlinghetti

I am waiting, Lawrence
to hear the chime of bells singing a
Hallelujah not predicated on Dogma—
I am waiting to hear peals of pure joy
I am waiting for the other shoe to fall
I am waiting
for a nuanced whisper to awaken my ancestors
and I am waiting
for the wails of mothers to stop
Mothers who cannot feed their newborns
Mothers who carry shattered bodies of children
I am waiting
for the moans of raped and abused women to cease
and I am waiting
for batterers and rapists to repent for their cruelty
and deadhead the cycle of abuse
I am waiting
for the chimes that will synch peril and war, and,
without retribution, to sink the ship of Authority
I am waiting for Godot
I am waiting, too,
for the wings of Anarchy to beat with fervor,
to sail into the ravenous open mouth of history,
to invite crisp air into a realm of harmony

I am waiting
for the cows to come home
I am waiting
for people to concede that paintball and football
are inherently warfare, and I am waiting
for the liberation of all animals, even insects
I'm waiting for the postman to ring once

I am waiting
for poverty to stop gnawing at the guts of
nearly a million earthlings, and I am waiting
for Big Mama in the desert to lay out an Elysian banquet
for the world
I am waiting, also, for Mami Wata to bathe all residents
of the planet in a bas-relief of delight
I am waiting
for workers in mines to strike forever and for windmills
and solar panels to sing the body electric
I am waiting
for an opera of galactic harmony

An Island in the Mind

Geoffrey Heptonstall

High winds are coming down the coast
with bitter rain that falls as snow
in the vicinity of Sacramento.
We know where the cause lies
among favours to friends
in unelected affinities
that ravage the earth for gold.
We see the work of the worst,
whether or not we know why
the world is changing by the hour.

The time is to walk down
an avenue of optimism,
seeking the signs of harmony
among rumours of the future.
We find behind the hidden door
an island in the mind,
the city that lives within
those who follow the sound
of the rivers that flow
from the days of rage and love.

Never will the world be gone
while what we imagine moves
in our opening mind.
And a new moon risen
not yet trespassed
in dreaming reality
of a lyre in the wind,
of a page turning,
of the final chapter,
the one that is unending.

Poetic Archetypes

Adrian Arias

I am waiting
for Alice in Wonderland
to retransmit to me
her total dream of innocence
"I Am Waiting"—Ferlinghetti

1
What exists
lives inside what did not exist,
what does not exist
lives within the possibility.

2 (to break the # 1)
Possibility lives within doubt,
the impossible also lives there.
In doubt
the possible and the impossible
are inseparable brothers
who play without knowing that they are,
until one has to leave
and abandon the other.

3
The unreal and the imaginary were best friends
until one day the reality
interposed.

4
The table is still a table
with one, two, three, or four legs.
We brothers are like that
we're just not so good

maintaining the balance
with what we have to do.

5
A couple kisses,
a person kisses in the mirror.
In each case there are two people in each scene.
In one case there is an interaction with an illusion
in the other case
the illusion is the interaction.

to be a poet

silvi alcivar

I

as with humans, poems have fatal flaws.

three minutes or less. no editing or revision. for better or for worse.

II

be a teller of great tales, even the darkest.

the tales that cast shadows on my life: my father's death, my mother's cancer. these are the stories i will forever be writing. note: you cannot have shadow unless you have light.

III

think long thoughts in short sentences.

secrets are safe in whale songs. sisters in pirate stores need mopping. fog sits haunting. the best part is best. trust strangers to mail your mail. alamo square will teach you wind. trouble sings like hummingbird wings. gratitude fuels greatness. sometimes birds poop on benches. make time for yes. no. oh. yes.

IV

the sunshine of poetry casts shadows, paint them too.

secrets you never told anyone: putting his toothbrush in the toilet. giving the homeless man a dollar most days. telling another you can't spare any change. how it felt to be caught. how it felt to be saved. loving the girl with the apron. trying to jump off the bridge. hugging him. getting married. knowing we will never see each other again.

V

if you have to teach poetry, strike your blackboard with the chalk of light.

i am teaching them imitation. we read nikki giovanni and they utter, ooo's. old enough to be grandparents, sometimes great ones, they are from el salvador, the philippines, jamaica, the united states of america, have been to turkey, japan, but mostly, have lived here, in san francisco. we count up the years: 503 collectively.

VI

allow yourself dazzling flight—flights of imagination.

i will not wait to become a bird. already i find feathers between the sheets of my bed, dark, iridescent. contrast the sharp yellow eye of a starling, a mallard's wing, a peacock's lady-getters. this morning ravens collected shiny things in my bedroom and offered them at my feet, laughing, as if they too know what each night i am becoming.

VII

secretly liberate any being you see in a cage.

see especially prisons, nursing homes, hospitals, high school proms, zoos, and those without: faces, tongues, families, friends, happiness, truth, freedom from shame.

VIII

write short poems in the voice of birds.

the little black bird
sings like water dropping,
now pick up your jaw.

IX

if you call yourself a poet, sing it, don't state it.

my voice meets a stranger's and is recorded on the taptataptap of red royal typewriter keys. tell me what you sing. i am listening.

X

wake up, the world's on fire!

what more is there to say than this?

What is Poetry?

Michael Warr

after *What is Poetry?*—Ferlinghetti

Poetry is what the Gods created on the eighth day.
Poetry is the capture of fire in defiance of darkness.
Poetry is the radiant residue of silent storm clouds.
Poetry is language tripping accidentally off of our tongues.
Poetry is the Ancients' way of making us pay attention.
Poetry is the Village Crier revolting inside your mouth.
Poetry is the ridges on the trilobite and shores of Pangaea.
Poetry is the eruptive ripple at the center of an explosion.
Poetry is the magnifying glass in our collective eye.
Poetry is the heavenly exhalation of earthly revolutions.
Poetry is the shaman's trickery for seeing around corners.
Poetry is the periscope used to survey the unseen plane.
Poetry is the doorknob on our existential implosions.
Poetry is the trillion utterances trembling throughout existence.
Poetry is the cave entering our dark, damp, bodies.
Poetry is the act of soaking in the sun — forever.
Poetry is the deciphering of death's aftermath.
Poetry is the ecstasy of unexpected ejaculation.
Poetry is the pitch-black star-lit universe above Mali's desert.
Poetry is the sentient drone spying on humanity.
Poetry is the movement of moons, symphonies, bowels, and time.
Poetry is the unknown poet's pyramid erected for the Afterlife.
Poetry is the unforgettable balm your mother gave you.

Poetry is the resurrection of assassinated hope.
Poetry is the event horizon to all that we have lost.
Poetry is the scaffolding surrounding our floating souls.
Poetry is the child addicted to eternal questions.
Poetry is the elixir of the city where I first imagined.
Poetry is the self-imposed evidence of insatiable longing.
Poetry is Patricia in satin blue wandering through Chicago's snow.
Poetry is the Colibri Hummingbird dancing on magnetic currents.
Poetry is the incessant search for another word for love.
Poetry is the endless attempt to explain the inexplicable.
Poetry is the molecule clinging to all atoms of art.
Poetry is the meticulous peeling of Neruda's onion.
Poetry is the alchemy of turning syllables into survival.
Poetry is the power of pedestrian language chosen carefully.
Poetry is the obsession with an uncontrollable act of telling.
Poetry is the condensation of the cosmos into metered meaning.
Poetry is the organic pulsing machinery for making memory.
Poetry is the "Pool Players" "Seven" in the hands of a book thief.
Poetry is the most loving way to describe a loaf of bread.
Poetry is the cyclical trance induced by Coltrane's "Impressions."
Poetry is the relentless reckoning with unrelenting oppression.
Poetry is the fulcrum for upending the earth.
Poetry is what the Archangel says it is.

Poetry is . . .

What Poetry Is
An Ars Poetica Cento as Villanelle

Andrena Zawinski

after *What is Poetry?*—Ferlinghetti

Poetry is a river many voices travel,
a sigh at dawn, a wild soft laughter
that carries us from this mortal world.

It is all things born with wings that sing,
made with the syllables of dreams.
Poetry is a river many voices travel.

It is far, far cries upon a beach at nightfall,
a lighthouse moving its megaphone over the sea.
Poetry carries us from this mortal world.

It speaks the unspeakable,
utters the unutterable sigh of the heart.
Poetry is a river many voices travel.

Poetry is the sun streaming in meshes of morning,
the boat moored in shade at the bend of the river
that carries us from this mortal world.

Poetry is a humming, a keening, a laughing
dissolving halos in oceans of sound
on a river many voices travel
that carries us from this mortal world.

A Little Over 6000 Years Ago

Kenneth Pobo

> And give us new dreams to dream,
> Give us new myths to live by!
> "To the Oracle at Delphi"—Ferlinghetti

Adam pops out
from behind a crabapple tree,
in bloom of course, everything
always blooming. Nothing dies.
He says he wants to have sex
which will be perfect because
he's perfect, I'm perfect,
and we'll both enjoy it perfectly
before we eat perfect food
that God provides. It's tasty,
but I get a yen for forbidden fruit--
I'll bet it's perfect too. I pick some
and hand it to Adam who takes it
perfectly well. Oh my, we're naked.
He sees this too. Our imperfections
run under ferns like mice.
God is angry and perfect.
After we get expelled, Adam wants
sex again. He doesn't even ask.
He's the only game in town. I wish
God would quit watching us.
We have discovered privacy.

Attraction

Jack Prizmich

> Great Oracle, why are you staring at me,
> do I baffle you, do I make you despair?
> "To the Oracle at Delphi"—Ferlinghetti

That small rock in my shoe,
Where did that come from?
And exactly when did that bougainvillea
Get so red? That rose pink?
That lavender blue?
Each thing attracted to its
Own color and calling
A child to kindness, winter to white
Obsidian to sharp glassy black
An artist to beauty, a pen to clean paper
A squirrel to a nutty tourist
And all of us to the sun
The stars and the galaxies
Every molecule and every movement
To the relentless law of gravity
Ignorance or obsession will not change a
Nano bit of it
A forked stick holds up the blossoming
Peach tree branch
Our astrologer friend with large, calloused
Hands, lensless glasses
And endless, soulful soft-spoken stories
Carefully, considerately sifts dirt for the garden

Bad Student

Marc Petrie

after Ferlinghetti's translation of *Paroles* by Jacques Prévert

His face says no!
Even as his heart says please.
He texts those he likes
On his cellphone under the desk
Even as the teacher glares.
He gets up to sharpen his pencil
In the middle of a lesson
And when the teacher questions his movement
He howls with derision as he cranks the handle
To sharpen his pencil to a nub.
He mocks the algorithms, the numbers, the words, the rules
Even as the maestro writes them on the white board.
He makes his way to the board
As the good students shout SIT DOWN,
He grabs all four board markers
Blue, green, red, and black
Then draws a magnificent multicolor mural
Over the sterile white background.

Candy

Ron. Lavalette

A cat upon the counter moved among
the licorice sticks
A Coney Island of the Mind, 20—Ferlinghetti

I'd like to live upstairs from a candy store.
Over the years, I've read a few great poems
about life amid candy:
Just this morning,
on my reluctant drive to work, I stopped
at the rest area and read all about how
Pinsky wakes up with his new love, looks down
at the sweetshop's wrinkled awning, watches
an early fog lifting to reveal pigeons pecking
at rainbowed gutters;
and the venerable
Ferlinghetti, ages and ages ago, wrote about
falling in love with unreality amid licorice and
jellybeans on a gloomy September afternoon
in the pennycandystore beyond the El.
Decades
later, sometime in my early twenties, a baby
poet, I vowed that I'd pitch a tent outside
Munson's Kandy Kitchen, and live on chocolate
and peanut butter eggs.
I'm not so old, nor
blind, now, looking back, to see I should have
kept that vow.

About 7 (Reconfigured)

Susana H. Case

after "Yes" (*Pictures of the Gone World,* 7)—Ferlinghetti

And
a dancing harlequin stood
in among the naked
nursemaids when they should have
been picking up
coins in the
Central Park
fountains their noses dropping and
yes we came and caught

them

Lunch Poem

Richard Landers

Stop
The oldest word in the book
But urgent, and could not be more
Contemporary every time. Yes,

Likely the most positive word
Ever to spill over a page
In English, and would you agree
In any language?

We can play language
Tricks all day but now that I have you
Tell me what your favorite color is?
White or red?

And should the tickling be with a rose
Or the tip of a faux beaver fur?
The sort that would have plunged the French
Deep into the Parc Gatineau

In search of inestimable pelts
Dried treated massaged
And put in a gold case
For the eyes of the nouveau riche

Alone. If only I could bottle
The sherry color of your eyes
Then drink only to them
As the forward slant of time

Bumps up against my erotic passages,
Proving
At long last that first thought
Is sexual.

Avant-garde is one way to look ahead
Just be sure
Your bark is as big as your undeniable

Sombrero.

If I'm going to read lunch poems,
Sure as hell I'll write one. Pour
A glass of Douro to remember
Your bold dark ecstasy

But memory fails, is faulty, you know . . .
You're here
Why not pull draw
Drink from the live well & swoon

The nectar of the blooming wreath
Garland rose so sweet
I put it under an umbrella to hide
So passing voyeurs wouldn't adjust journey,

Course-correct their misguided path,
An eclipsed corner of High Street
With just enough space to spout
And roll

Over on my side & dream.
Finally to the eye exam & coming out
To the sunny afternoon hungry for lunch
Like walking into a Monet painting at 1 o'clock

Blinded by light on 57th Street
Ducked into a 5 and 10 for a cheap pair
Of shades
Hoping for more beauty

The casual light in Central Park perhaps
Reflected
In a pool and Cleopatra's
Needle standing high

Above the crowds
Erect and in complete control

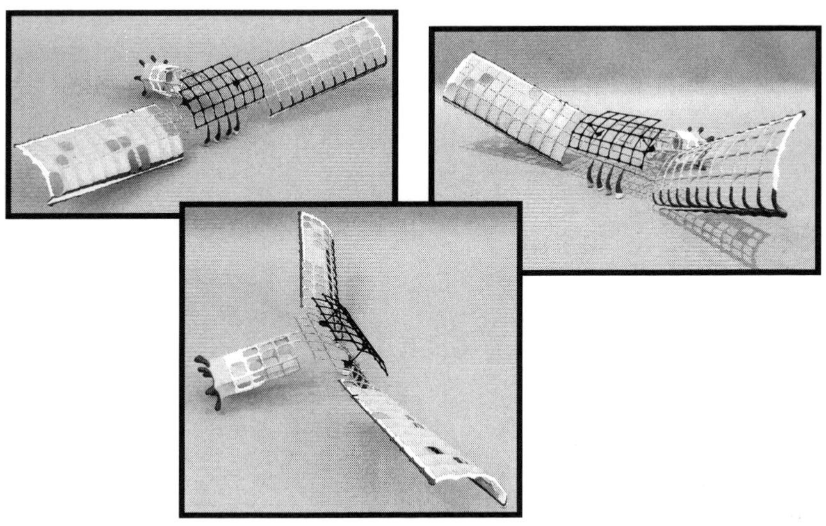

And the Wright brothers said they thought they had invented
something that could make peace on earth
(if the wrong brothers didn't get hold of it)

"History of the Airplane"—Ferlinghetti

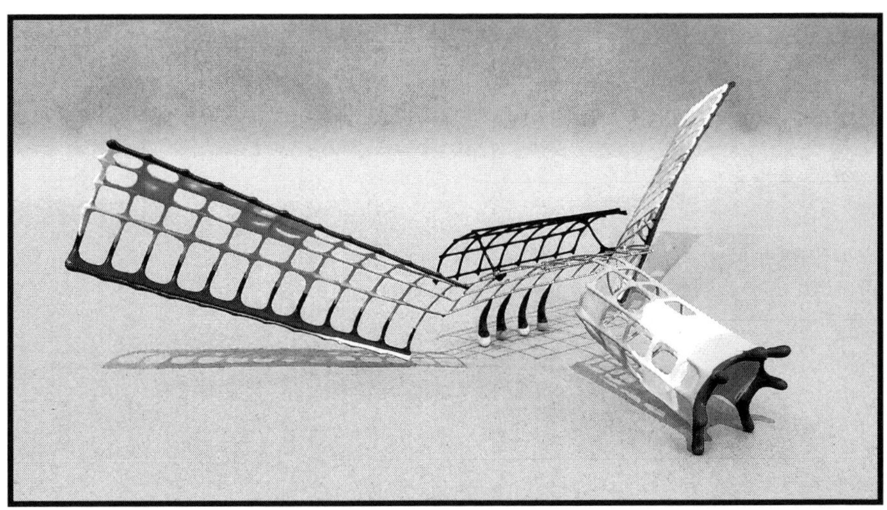

Open the Bomb Bay Doors, Hal **Richard Alpert**
3" x 16" x 6" steel wire, fabric, synthetic rubber, 2020
Created in direct response to reading "History of the Airplane"

Workdays

Susana H. Case

Sometimes on the Q train, I'm tempted
to stay all the way to the end of the line,
Coney Island, riding with commuters
desperately clutching Starbucks cups
under cement skies, to where love lies, where

I might walk barefoot on sand, peel oranges,
or eat Russian vareniki with fried onions,
and watch the old people sun themselves
to crinkled ruin, semi-naked on a boardwalk
that has too many nails

poking up through rotten boards.
A metaphor for this world, and yes,
things are awful in the world, and it's hard
not to despair, even when the ocean rolls in,
the cathedral-like ocean,

a part of it that isn't perpetually sad
from having to embrace dead children,
a part that doesn't look like a print from
The Disasters of War.
Goya never wrote about his intentions

in making *The Disasters of War*—it wasn't safe.
What can artists and poets say except:
Look at what we've done in this world we run,
our Wonder Wheel of humanity,
ever sliding off the rails between hub and rim.

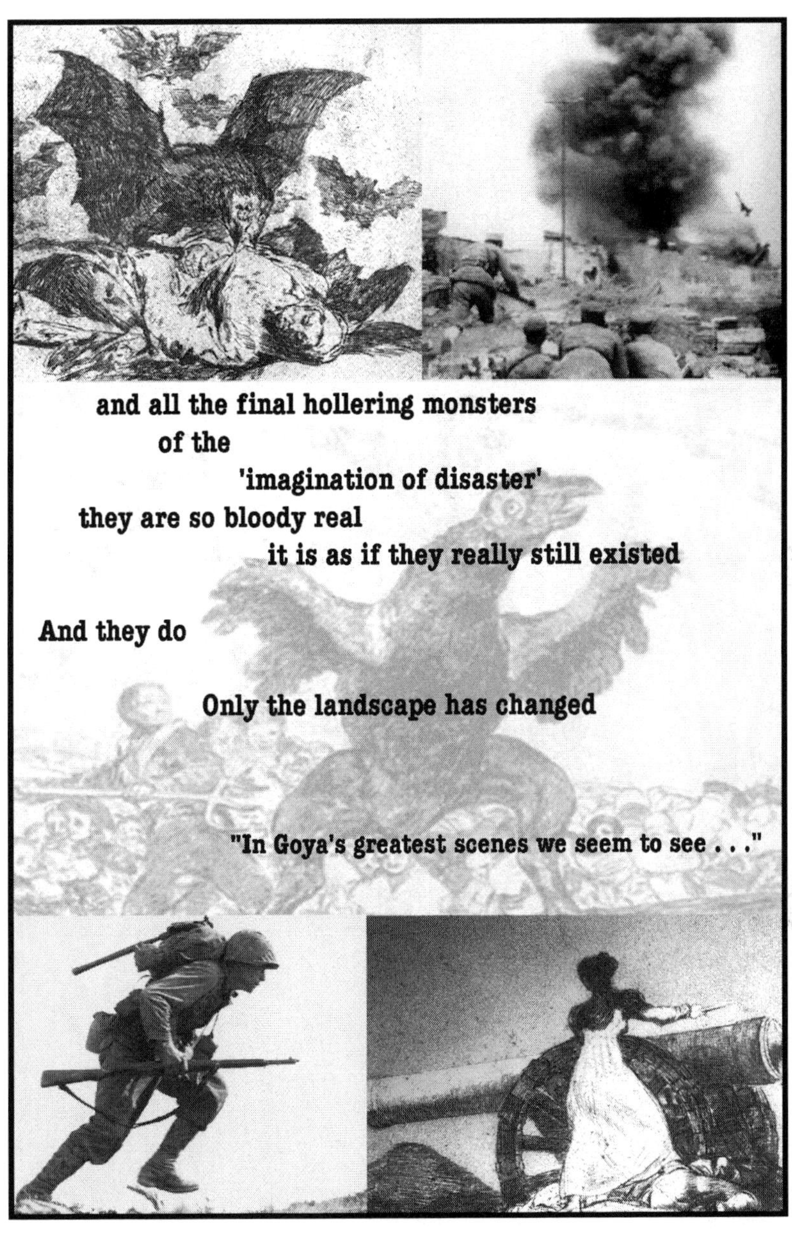

Francisco Goya created his 82-print series *The Disasters of War* (*Los desastres de la guerra*) between 1810-1820. As a 26-year-old navigator in the U.S. Navy, Ferlinghetti entered Nagasaki just weeks after the atomic bomb was dropped. Witnessing the horrific devastation, he became a lifelong pacifist.

Boat People

Kelliane Parker

after Ferlinghetti's *Boat People* (painting, 2006)

I remember running on the beach
In another life
But have since forgotten the firmness of land
The tenuousness of sand
The firmness of soil
Slipping, shifting sand
Transitions us to
To thin boards beneath us
And fluid buoyancy

I am a buoy
I am a boy
I am a bobbing boat
To an unknown destination
Bobbing and rocking
Holding fierce to the view of shore
To return to land
No, not my land
But a place to land, in another land
The first unsafe, the other safer

A land I do not know
But the stars do
The only thing I carry from home

Passing invisible meridians
Under familiar skies
Waiting, for a sign,
you are here
Waiting, to return to land
A place to land
Now, my land

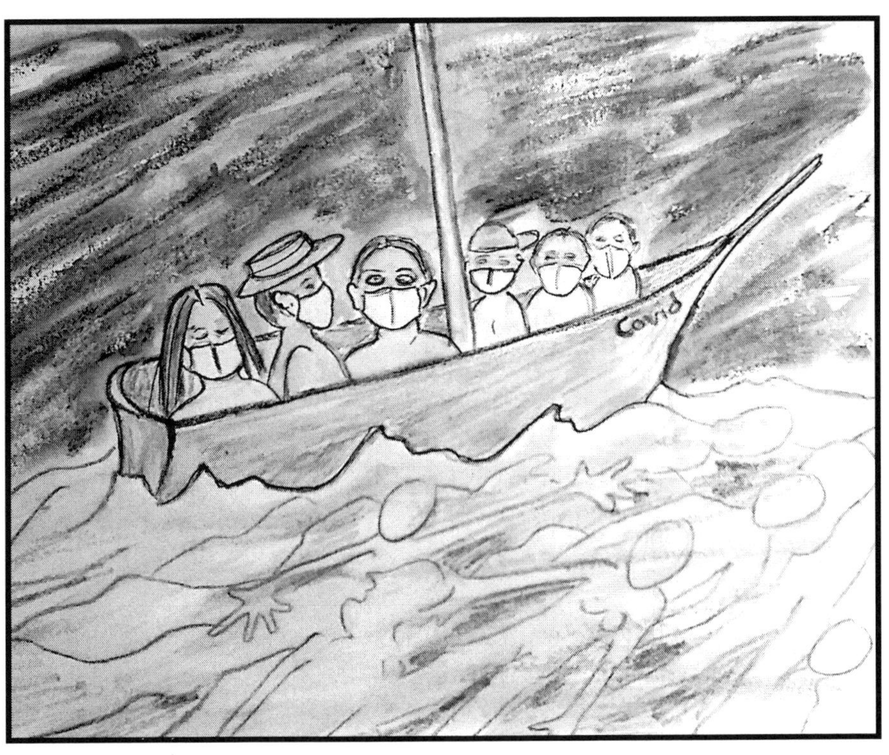

We're All in the Same Boat **Virginia Barrett**
after Ferlinghetti's *Boat People*, 2006
10" x 12" mixed media on paper, 2020

Reading Ferlinghetti During the Pandemic
a pantoum-cento

Sandra Anfang

My country tears of thee
thou shalt not kill except by complicity
the perfect picture of a monarchy
where beauty stands and waits with gravity.

Thou shalt not kill except by complicity
the world is a beautiful place to be born into
where beauty stands and waits with gravity
and there are no strings attached.

The world is a beautiful place to be born into
if you don't mind happiness not always being so much fun
and there are no strings attached
trying to recall something forgotten.

If you don't mind happiness not always being so much fun
a thousand threaded images of light
trying to recall something forgotten
between language and reality.

A thousand threaded images of light
constantly risking absurdity
between language and reality
and nobody the wiser.

Constantly risking absurdity
as if they were finally questioning existence
and nobody the wiser
everyone wondering where and how it will end.

As if they were finally questioning existence
my country tears of thee
everyone wondering where and how it will end where beauty
stands and waits with gravity.

Mute Poets

Paola Corso

after "Blind Poet"—Ferlinghetti

(to be performed while wearing a surgical mask)

No sitting on a stoop—
Phyllis steps above,
Gabriella steps below,
me in the middle.

The Ferlinghetti Girls are furloughed.

We've suspended
our *Zuppa Nella Stoopa*
open mics where we make
a pot of soup to share
on Phyllis' stoop,
send loving barbs from bards
to neighbors passing by
as we toast with Prosecco,
lick luscious lips
made by the chocolatier.
I bought bunches of escarole
and cans of cannelloni
for Italian greens and beans
but they're on ice
in the big freeze
ever since the cad isn't
with his caddie on the green,
isn't railing away at rallies
and let the doctor step
up to the mic to speak science.
Our bunny baskets were filled
with hand-sewn masks
the color of eggshell blue,
pink peeps, and jellybean cheer.
We're not boardwalking our poems
in our stay-at-home state,

wondering where
our next roll of toilet paper
is coming from,
baking too many cookies
and reading about a dutiful son
standing in a bucket truck
three flights up
outside his elderly mother's
nursing home window
so he can visit with her.

Furloughed

Ferlinghetti Girls who've got
his Coney Island of the mind.
Our voices penetrate
polypropylene plastic,
voices loud enough
to blow your house down
as mother poet
Maria Mazziotti Gillan would say,
voices in three-part harmony
of our Italian American experience
as women who don't wave
wooden spoons to get you to *mangia*,
but stitch and stitch and stitch
like garment workers embroidering
our stories together,
sharing the same seam

as   we   sing.
Aswesing.

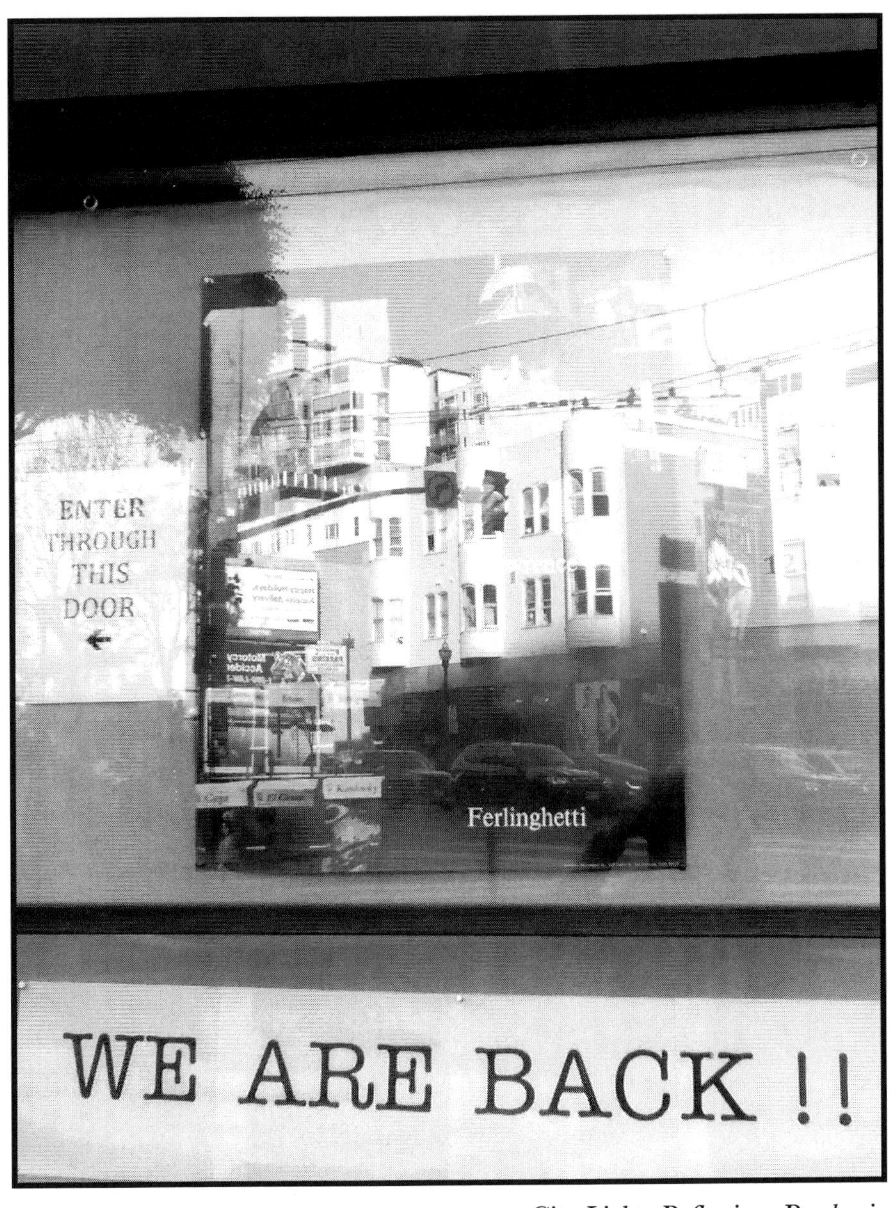

City Lights Reflection: *Pandemic*
December, 2020

Remembering "In Golden Gate Park that Day . . ."

Karen Melander-Magoon

On Mason Street two people are walking
The street is empty
But two people walk
One has two paper sacks and wears a jacket
The other is dressed in grey shorts and a black sweatshirt
And carries a bunch of grapes
The street is empty
Empty because of a virus
I look down on the street
From a wire
Like a trapeze artist
I think I could look up at the street
From the gutters
Drowning in absurdity
Yet seeing green suspenders
Walking down the street
With no one inside

2

Tidings

The sunshine of poetry casts shadows. Paint them too.

Poetry as Insurgent Art—Ferlinghetti

Poem for Ferlinghetti

Matthew Zapruder

Everything I know about birds
is I can't remember plus
two of the four mourning
also known as rain
doves, the young ones
born in my back yard
just this April. I saw
them moving their wings
very rapidly in a back
and forth motion
particular to their species.
Monica said it means
they want to be fed.
Their parents are likely
deeper in the stand
of trees being careful.
The wind has a metal hand.
Around them the city
explodes with helicopters
and tourists but here
on Francisco Street where
you also live this yard
is protected but not quiet.
I can hear the Russian
woman talking out
the window, I catch
a few words, one
of which sounds like
"object force." It makes
me think of Anna
who is probably married
to that Finnish Brazilian
martial arts instructor.
That was afternoon.
Now it is later,
much, the absolute

worst pure center
of night, for an hour
in bed I resisted coming
here to my desk
to search for those terrible
destructive questions still
hiding from me.
Do you do that? Or
is there some other way?
I thought I might
but I can't see
the yard at all, just
some yellow safety
lights in the alley. I try
to keep the chair
from creaking, I know
Sarah knows in her sleep
I am in my study,
disturbed. I wish
I could send the word
asylum out very far
into the air like a clear
colorless substance
all my friends could
breathe in sleep, you
can never protect
everyone. That constant
humming sound is time
coming to take us
away from each other.
Or the refrigerator,
keeping the milk cold
and pure. So much
noise all the time
in the city, do you like it?
You must, you stay.
Last week I limped
in my giant ridiculous cast
one block to get coffee

on the corner and sat
outside feeling very sorry
but also happy. You
sat next to me and I was
pretty sure you
were you but I didn't
know. I gave you
my *New York Times*
and we talked about torture
and baseball and how
many more weeks
are left for newspapers.
And then you asked me
if I'd ever be able to walk again.
That's what it's like
to be eighty I thought
but I don't know. Nothing's
natural to me anymore.
I forgot to buy a light bulb.
Now in the afternoon
the blades of grass
are completely still. No one
tends a little television
in the Russian woman's window.
All I know is I have tried
for a long time to be useful,
like everyone I am also
always balancing
on the small blade of not
letting other people down.
Now it is getting darker.
Orange nasturtiums
you can go out and gather
and place directly into a salad
are glowing, and pink
roses wander along
the very old green wooden
trellis towards the blue shed
where Ephraim carefully traces

his engineering plans
for great structures
that will never be built
at least in the few
decades of his lifetime
remaining. He walks
with a little hunch towards
me to collect my rent
check and I am holding it
out to him both of us
with matching apologetic smiles.
In Oklahoma once
I ate blueberries, I
recall they tasted like lake.
If dust is particles
of our skin why
is there more each
time I return?
I know tomorrow
I will sit in that dark
before daylight without
a name, and feeling
the last few drops
of water from the shower
still on her shoulders
she will come and stand
next to me where I am
at my desk pushing
against one word feeling
its hinge creak like wind
would a gate if it could feel
anything at all.

The Poet

Jeffrey Grossman

after *Back Roads to Far Places*—Ferlinghetti

The poet with no lock on love speaks.
His voice the directness of a touch.
His touch the sound of the beat of his heart.
That we live by what he says he prays not
But by touch the sound of the beat of the heart.

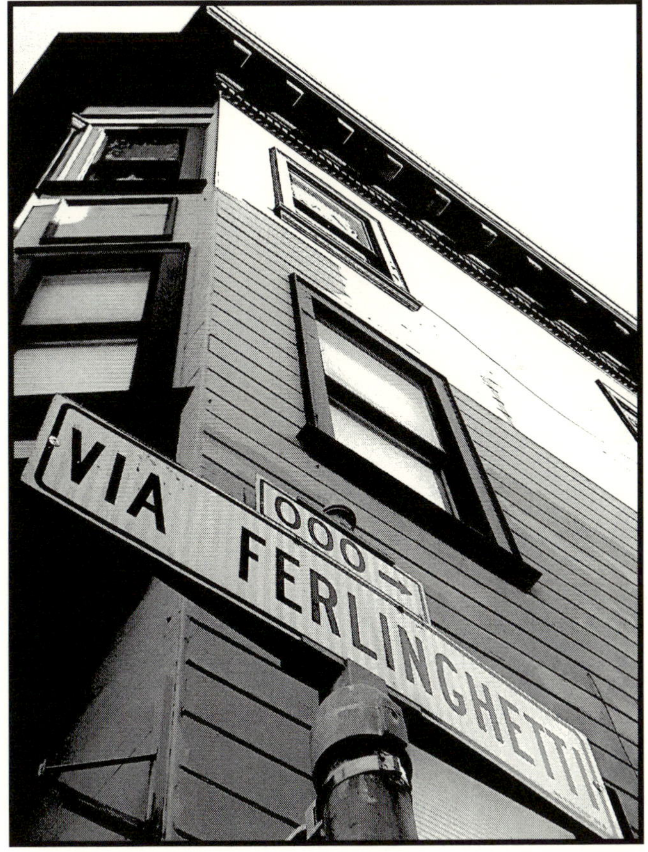

Via Ferlinghetti
North Beach, San Francisco

The Ferlinghetti School of Poetics

Joan Gelfand

> *All* that we see or seem
> Is but a dream within a dream.
> "A Dream within a Dream"—Edgar Allan Poe

I: The dream within the dream within the dream

What is it, Ferlinghetti,
Taking star turns in my dreams?
Strolling in front of cars
Haunting alleyways, stairways,
Bars? Beating moth-like flitting through
San Francisco's sex-fraught avenues? In North Beach
Where XXX marks art and
Nasty commerce collide, intersect Columbus,
Telegraph Hill, Jack Kerouac Way.
You are fog whispering in from the sea
On another sunny day.

There's a breathless hush on the freeway tonight /
Beyond the ledges of concrete / restaurants fall into dreams /
with candlelight couples / Lost Alexandria still burns

Ferlinghetti's words sink, weighted
On the business end of an invisible fishing line,
Dredging last night's dream to the surface, gasping for air
Shivering like some catfish
Eyes bulging, wet lake water dripping off its scales.
The knife of memory slices open
That dream, finds me on haunted streets,
Instructing a small boy:
"You gotta go to the Ferlinghetti school. It's totally rad
and completely cool."

II: Ferlinghetti Makes an Appearance

Phantom audience shouts: "Higher! Higher!"
Egg the poets on—after all, they're not on the wire.

Higher? We spin the memory wheel until there's my father
Strolling through his own Coney Island
And there he is again winning a goldfish.
The clerk hands it over fish circling in plastic bag.
Big Daddy pretends
It's all for the kids.
He needed to win like that fish needed water.

III: The Poet Reconsiders

Is the skill of life just keeping on
All the gears oiled, the doors open?
Even if the past keeps drowning and the knifed open
Dream fish still swims around?

In dream theater Ferlinghetti arrives.
Was it the Regal, the Royal or the Metreon?
I rise to make room for he who started everything
Got the wheel of poetry turning, broke
Open language, letters. Vaporized
While he drifts
Haunting my dreams.

Fortune
has its cookies to give out
A Coney Island of the Mind—Ferlinghetti

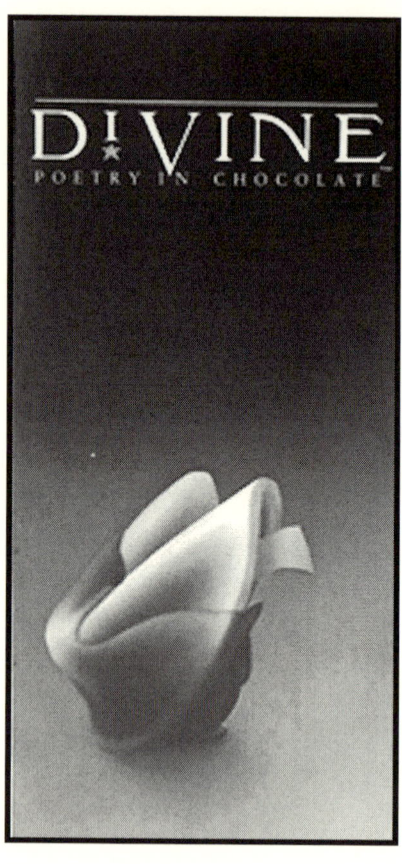

Lawrence generously gave permission for his words from *A Coney Island of the Mind* to lead an artist-led business venture in New York. In alliance with the National Arts & Business Council I launched DIVINES, a reinvention of fortune cookies. With poetry in place of a fortune, and dipped in chocolate, they were sold nationally at retailers from Neiman-Marcus to Dean & DeLuca. For the first time, poetry readings were held in department stores with hundreds of writers including Gwendolyn Brooks, Allen Ginsberg, and Lawrence Durrell joining to raise funds for the arts in 1985.

Annice Jacoby

Principle of Double Reflection

Tamsin Spencer Smith

> "Young man, you've been to school—who was Telemachus?"
> *Little Boy*—Ferlinghetti

Boy sails off to learn something from the islands of old kings
Unsure of wayward arrows until the captive face of war
Tells him what she knows of silver tongues and homecoming
It is the nature of women to fill white sails
You will measure the angle of stars by line break
In his palm five moons bed at the finger base
One hand waxing
Revolution from the left
Each phase a new sea
A wave may melt the ice
Heart fills with what the mind casts off
You cannot touch the bottom of this journey
A center must hold itself
Make shelter for the stranger
From seaweed
A spine a masthead
The greatest beauty in the known world
Whispers through the kindling of a mighty hull
But you have never been afraid of words
Launched to light
Thousands upon thousands
Unflagged unsinkable

There is only one here
in the end as in beginning
one body breathing
one body singing

"I Am You"—Ferlinghetti

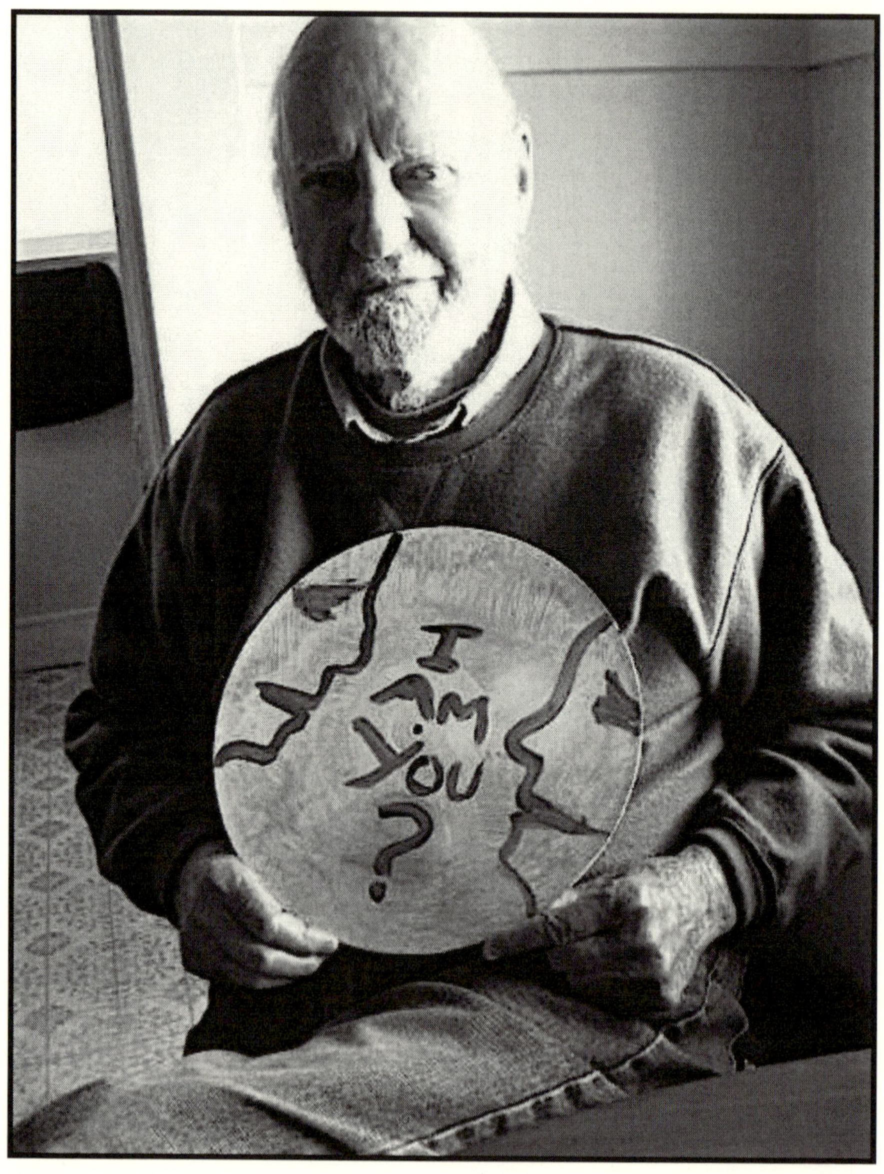

Lawrence in his Apartment I, 2014 **Soheyl Dahi**

One Day

Soheyl Dahi

Out of bed
Poetry in my veins
Coffee on my mind
In the car
Listening to Leonard Cohen
Zigzagging the streets
To North Beach
On to Francisco Street
Park the car
At the door
10 o'clock sharp
Note pinned on the door:
"SOHEYL
I am at
Caffe Francisco"
3 more blocks to walk
There is a table in the corner
By the window
Sun pouring down
On pages of *NY Times*
And on the man with oversized sunglasses
He weakly raises one hand
Then looks down
At his watch
"You're 5 minutes late!" he says
"Good morning, Lawrence," I say
He nods smiling and motions me
To sit down

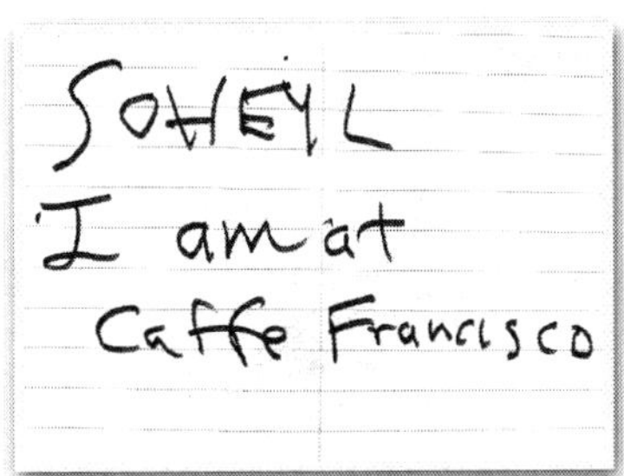
SOHEYL
I am at
Caffe Francisco

image of actual note

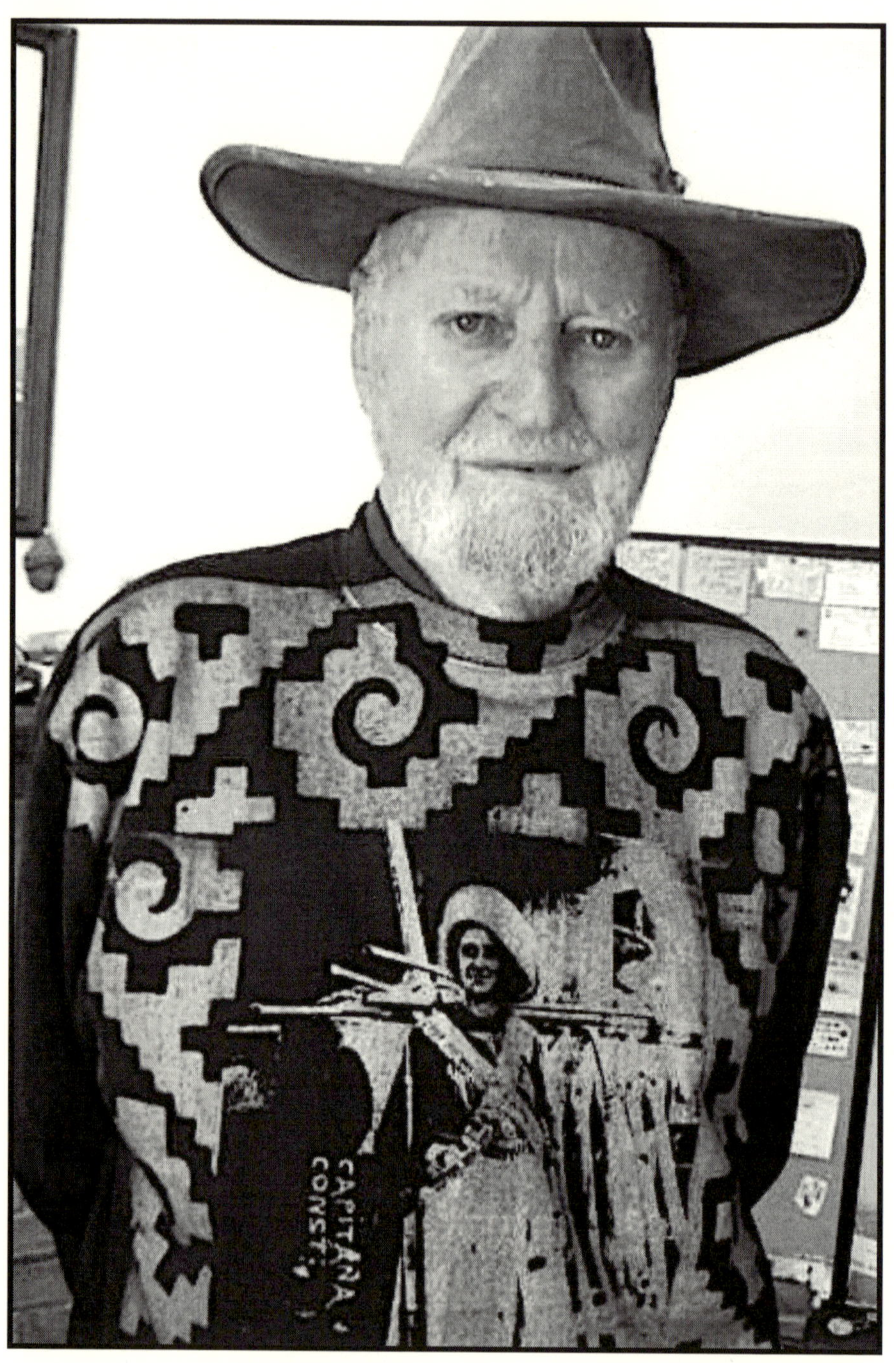

Lawrence in his Apartment II, 2014 **Soheyl Dahi**

Ferlinghetti at 97

Neeli Cherkovski

strolling down Columbus Avenue
to Little Joe's Restaurant
where we'd sit right before the flames
Lawrence in Greek sailor cap
my beret folded in my pocket

this is 1975 and there will be a heavy rain
soon enough—
there is Maria taking orders for lamb chops
and lasagna
we place our orders
the older cook will soon return
home to Italy

he places his cook's palm over one burner
high enough not to burn himself
and the flames rise
Lawrence breaks into a smile
and turns the decades
into a sentiment of words
that ring across San Francisco Bay
out to the open sea

"Ferlinghetti," a woman says
and he answers,
"No, I'm his twin brother—
the real one is at the bookstore
down the street
hiding behind a secret door"

the lights go on way up
on Walt Whitman's cloud
where he continues to dispense wisdom
and sleights-of-hand

while we eat the fire of the years
rises and falls

later we walk again
and he hands me the keys
to his Bixby cabin
"No coffee house there," he grins
"You have to make hobo coffee
over the fire
in the open pit"

then he is 97 years old
still the golden glow
of a man who landed at Normandy
and surveyed the fields of Nagasaki

still he wanders the streets
near *Notre-Dame*
and hides out in Mexico
and asks Apollinaire to join us
for dinner

the French poet shows up
forty-one years later
and takes a seat
in what is now
a vast Mycenaean dining room
where Edgar Allan Poe
coaxes a raven from the woods

A Coney Island of the Mind
was one of the books
I used to hide under my notebook
in math class at Arrowhead School

Lawrence is 97
the planet is a few decades older
it is 2016
and we need poesy

more than ever
in the heartless void
that has settled
on this cold spring morning

yeah, we offer gratitude
if only for the cabin and the poetry
and the library called City Lights
easily as massive as is
the Borges library
"The Library of Babel"

endless lunch, endless fire

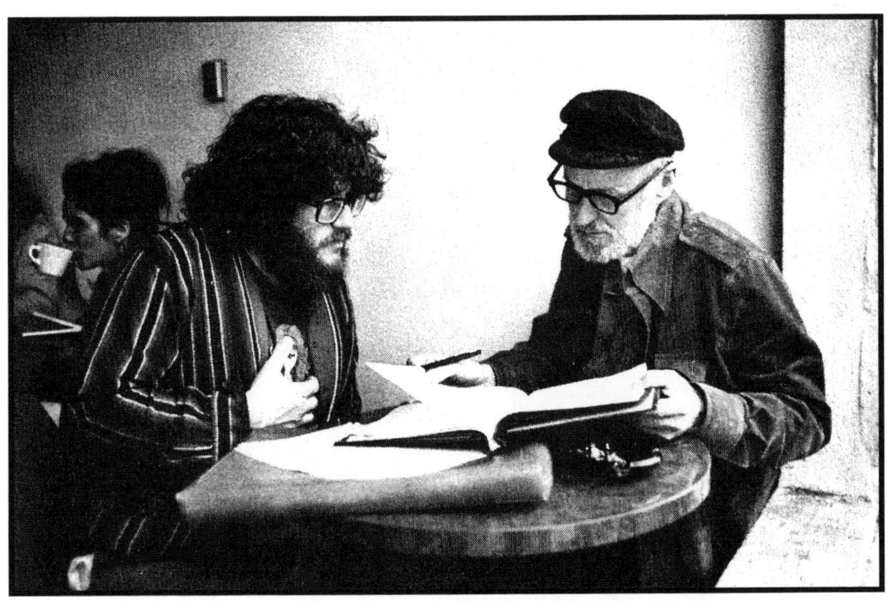

Cherkovski and Ferlinghetti **Ira Nowinski**
Savoy Tivoli, San Francisco, 1978

Ah Sun-flower! weary of time,
Who countest the steps of the Sun:
Seeking after that sweet golden clime
Where the travellers journey is done.
"Ah! Sun-flower"—William Blake

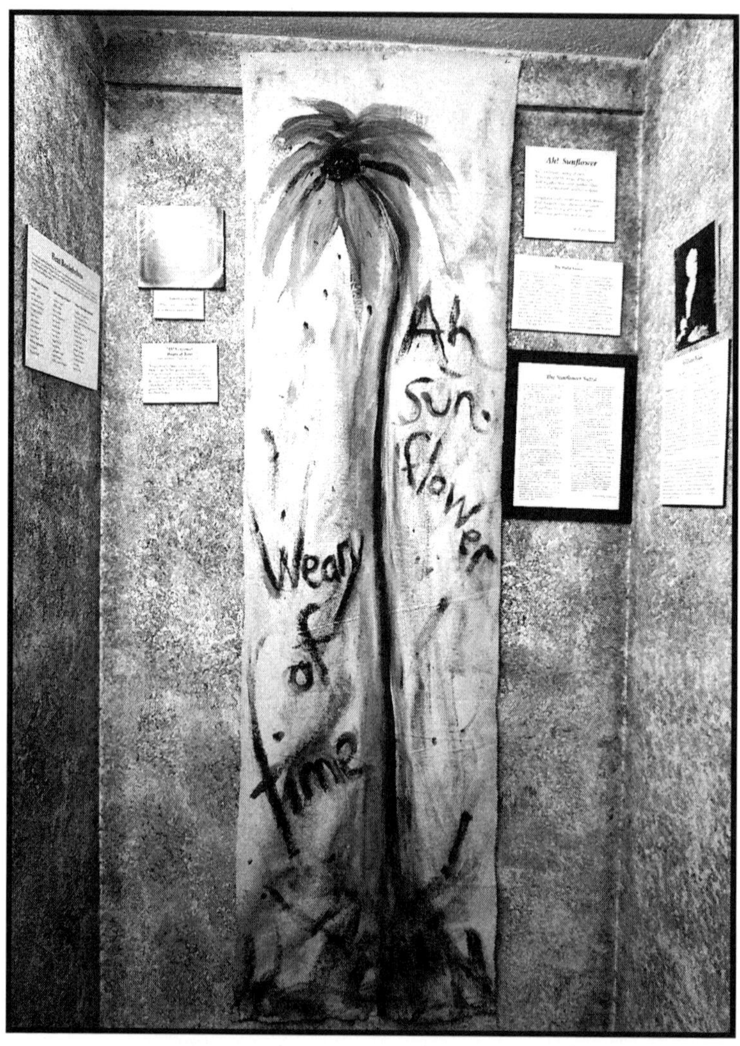

Ah Sun-flower, at the Beat Museum **Jerry Cimino**

Ferlinghetti's *Ah Sun-flower,* after William Blake's poem, is part of the permanent collection on view at the Beat Museum, San Francisco.

Ferlinghetti Memory

Jerry Cimino

Lawrence Ferlinghetti was the first poet I ever understood. City Lights is the reason I moved from Maryland to California. Lawrence is the reason I built The Beat Museum a mere 100 steps from Lawrence's office in North Beach.

The year was 1968. I was a 14-year-old in junior high school, witnessing the world turned upside down. Martin Luther King had been shot and killed in April. There were race riots in the streets of major American cities. Bobby Kennedy was killed in June. He was going to be President, and people all over America were yearning for a return to his brother's Camelot.

There were other troubles in 1968. There were protests in France, and Russian tanks were invading Czechoslovakia. My 14-year-old friends and I wondered, "What the hell are we inheriting?" as every night the evening news served up the horrors of Vietnam on our television sets. Our older brothers were receiving their draft notices in the mail, and we knew it would be but a brief period of time before our own notices came in the mail as well.

Into this mix, thanks to my eighth grade English teacher Mr. Schneider, came Lawrence Ferlinghetti. I was usually a cut-up in class. One time I was goofing so hard in the last row of English class with my friend Dan Rambo that Mr. Schneider literally threw a book at us. We watched in what seemed like slow motion as the large book sailed over our heads, striking the metal blinds of the window behind us with such a force and clatter we were afraid the glass had shattered.

Mr. Schneider seemed just the tiniest bit sheepish that he had lost his cool, but he didn't apologize. He simply looked us squarely in the eye, picked up another book, and said sternly, "Here's something you two goofballs might find interesting if you can pay attention long enough to try to understand it." And with a flourish he read to us Poem #5 from *A Coney Island of the Mind:*

Sometime during eternity
some guys show up
and one of them
who shows up real late
is a kind of a carpenter
from some square-type place
like Galilee
and he starts wailing
and claiming he is hip
to who made heaven
and earth
and that the cat
who really laid it on us
is his Dad . . .

I don't exactly remember if Dan had a reaction at that moment but I certainly remember I did. I had been raised Catholic, and even went to Catholic school for 5 years, and I was shocked to hear anyone speak about the crucifixion of Christ in such a casual and flippant manner. It was an instant revelation to me that the written word could come across so powerfully.

After that day in the eighth grade I soon forgot about Lawrence Ferlinghetti. I went off to high school, met a girl and soon had my first car, a 1965 Mustang convertible. A heartbeat later I was in college, meeting other girls and watching as the Vietnam War started to wind down. A week before I was to graduate college, my girlfriend at the time, desperate to get married for some unknown reason, dropped me like a hot potato when I resisted her rather strident hints, and quickly ran off to marry some other guy she barely knew. My heart was broken and I found myself doing the only respectable thing I could imagine someone in my situation might do . . . I started writing poetry.

Because I was new at it I thought, "If you're going to write poetry, you should probably read some poets." So I drove to my neighborhood bookstore, Towson Books, and after thumbing through the poetry section for a few minutes that poem from oh-so-long-ago leaped off the page: *Sometime during eternity / some guys show up . . .*

I immediately bought the book with my last dollar. A week later I came back with another dollar and bought *Scattered Poems* by Jack Kerouac, published by City Lights. A week after that it was *Howl* by Ginsberg. I had no idea that Ferlinghetti knew either Jack Kerouac or Allen Ginsberg, much less that he and City Lights had published them. I bought the books because they all had black and white covers and because F, G, & K were bunched together on the shelf.

Decades later, after I'd gotten to know Lawrence Ferlinghetti, I was speaking with him amongst friends at an art event and casually mentioned, "I was 14 years old when I first read *A Coney Island of the Mind*." Lawrence's blue eyes gleamed and he smiled an impish grin, and said to a friend we both knew: "That's when I get all of them. They're all 14 years old."

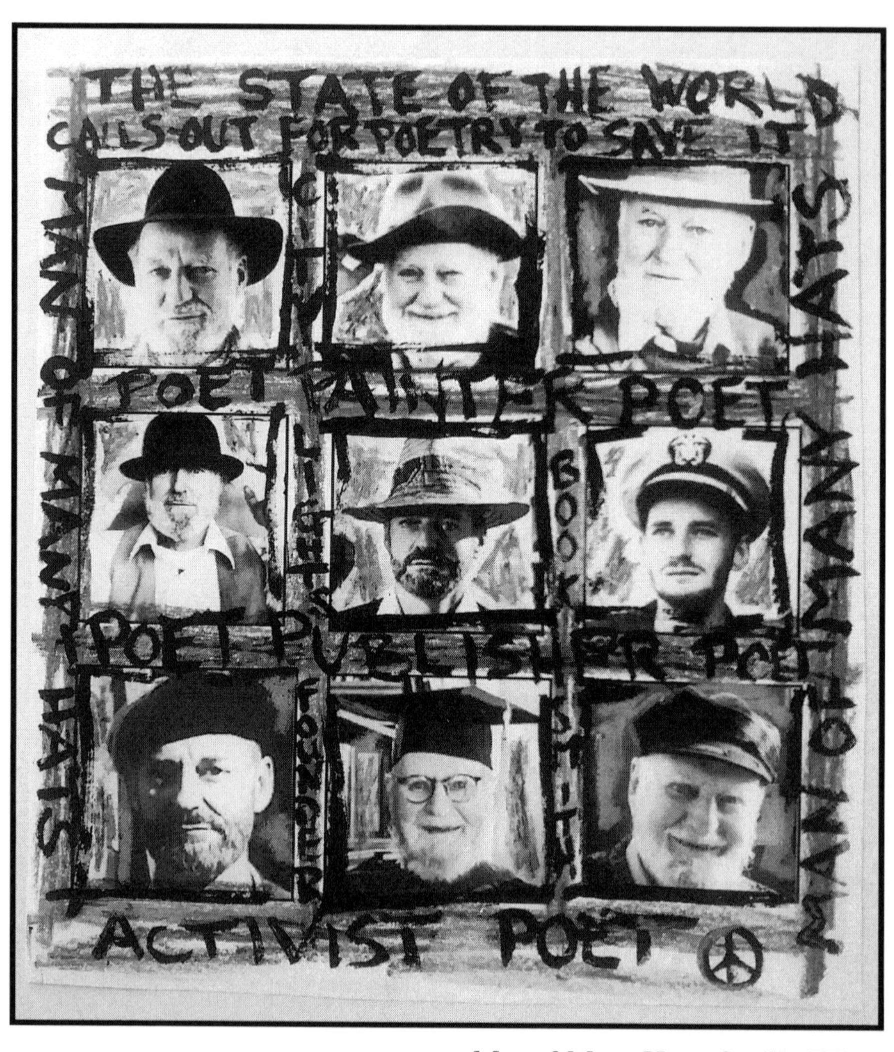

Man of Many Hats **Stella Klar**
9" x 12" mixed media on paper, 2020

Pop Hat

Jeffrey Grossman

> The door to the invisible
> is visible
> The hidden door
> is not hidden
> I walk through it forever
> not seeing it
> I am what I am
> And will be
> what I will be
>
> *Back Roads to Far Places*—Ferlinghetti

The hat worn by Joy much like the hat
Of Big Ben or the hat of Italian
Sausages spiced with Sophia Loren
And those limbs sifted through rays of sun
In fields of flowers gone wild is a hat
With trolleys full of abandoned dolls
Adept at being swept by the wind
While floating the h2o of canals
Through streets of old pals wearing hats that
Accused of smoke picnic faraway green
Where without wearing a hat one can dream
Like a hat from which curls drip to protect
A face from the sun in smiles that bark
Like runaway pups at the hems of dresses
Swirling in a tango of romance
Like the hat one doffs to a bride who salutes
A groom in a soldier hat undaunted
By widows yet moved by a hat from which
The huge sad ears of a tiny dog droop
Alas a horn blown hat The hat one would
Give to the face blushing sunset Yes
The hat that is the rose a dress becomes
When blown by the wind above the waist
Of hopscotch who skips like a stone over
Puddles of mud reflecting the hat
Worn by the news as well as the hat
No One wears because No One is *THERE*

Staring from a window at the hats
Of two loveless statues one of which is
Doomed to be hurled down the many flights
Of a curved stairway onto a floor
Where dust swirling settles in the core
Of a green apple that rolls into
An upside-down stovepipe that does not smoke
An urban farm gal hat A hat made
Of that which wears no hat A Ball Bowler
Borsalino Capone Cop Dick Tracy
Panama Pork Pie Skull Stetson Top hat
Often seen walking shellfish and beasts
Without a leash O hat of *qigong*!
With eyes of ping pong! A hat of distant
Light becoming even more distant as
The train it travels on travels beyond
The smoke it leaves behind O hat that protects
One from avalanche! An Indian headdress
A hat that *tossles* the cold A hat
That bathes the sun as it bathes in the sun
With a blade of grass between its teeth
Yes a revolutionary red black
A matador A monk hat that blows
The fleur-de-lis into the *Canon's* mouth!
That tattoos the fleur-de-lis in the hearts
And heads of sailors! Aye a sailor hat
Checkered by Italian tablecloths
And shadows cast by the sun behind bars
O dream hat of he who danced the Red Sea!
O derby! O sombrero of this green's
                Magnificent thoroughbred!

Manifesto

Indran Amirthanayagam

Let us be clear. There is no justice. And there is no memory.
The young have not read Ferlinghetti. The old are starting
to close their eyes reading the even older masters. This is
how Shakespeare has survived. At the end of the day,
when the tall and sleeping hill of books on the nightstand
blows its top—all the efforts of our best minds will
get burned up, except for the verses conserved beyond
the personal library, in homes and minds worldwide,
contemplating slings and arrows and the pearl richer
than all his tribe. But *A Coney Island of the Mind*
has sold more than a million copies, says the book jacket.
Who is keeping count? Poets in Southeast Washington DC
today, at the reading, did not know how Lawrence made
Howl circulate in the American democracy. But they have
heroes too, unconsulted except in school, Langston Hughes,
Zora Neale Hurston, Richard Wright. Let us bring the books
out of the bonfires and renew ourselves reading the old. Let us
not forget the ties that bind under that big, multi-colored tent.

Acrostic

JR Rhine

For a century or more now, we've
Entered this sweet skull whose
Recalcitrance has always been a
Lantern on these slick streets
Imagining myself a beat!
Now you might say,
Go with your ripe tongue into
Hell with all that nonsense,
Everyone's up for a little dying! I
Think, yes, Lawrence,
The world is a beautiful place; and
I don't think I much mind at all.

City of Poets

When Lawrence Became First San Francisco Poet Laureate

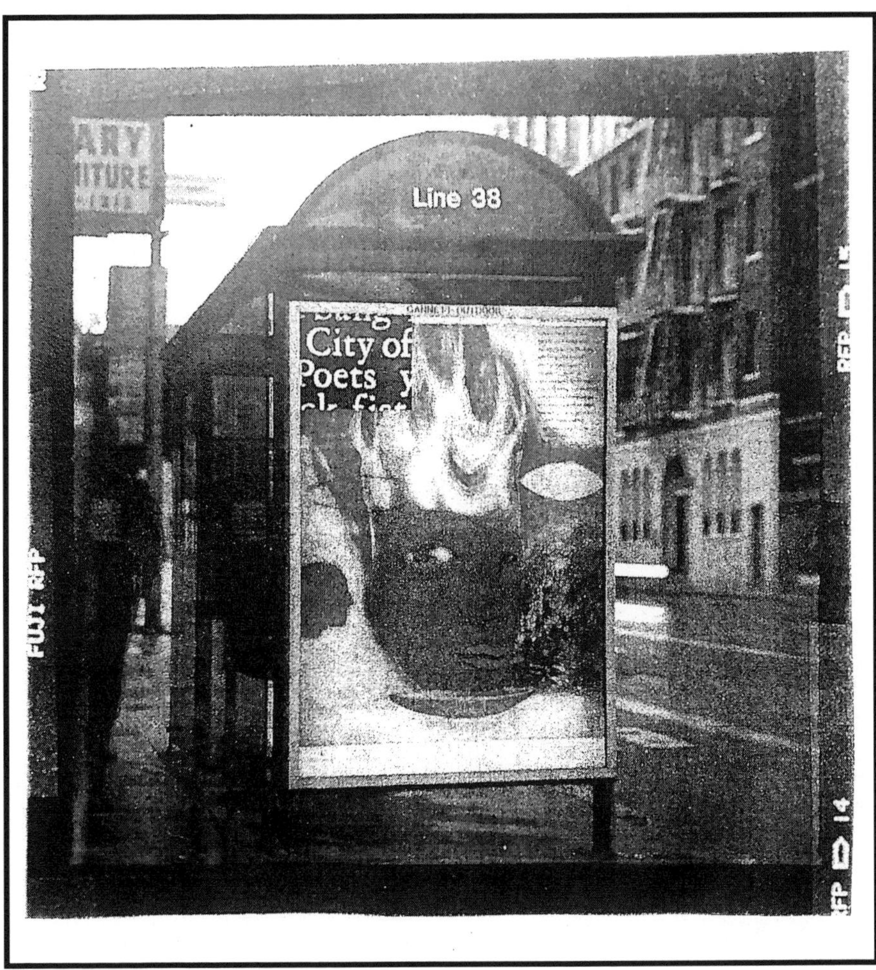

Launched in 1993, City of Poets showcased San Francisco's having a place for poetry in public life. Major events were produced in Union Square, in schools, and across the city. Hundreds of poets and community groups were involved including Allen Ginsberg opening a Giants game at Candlestick Park, Michael McClure on billboards, Jack Hirschman's homelessness poems displayed on supermarket shopping carts, Francisco X. Alarcón's invocations, a Maya Angelou celebration, and Neeli Cherkovski's coffeehouse series.

Annice Jacoby

The Ferlinghetti Arcane

Jack Hirschman

1.

Caro compagno, let's see,
how many years since we
first touched base?
Fifty, I believe (unless Al
Zheimer's already begun
playing tricks on me):
You'd come East early in
'61, riding the crest of the
Beat wave Jack and Allen
were out there drumming
on as a New American
Poetry, but you'd already
been internationaled in both
Atlantic and Pacific Ocean
theaters, chasing submarines
in the War and, after North
Carolina U. on the GI Bill,
getting your PhD in Paris
at the Sorbonne. That's one
of the synhar- monies always
reverberant between us: you
the consu- mate consonant
and vowel uttered, and I the
same vowel at the end of the
next syllable but only an
unsounded echo barely heard,
still being in the university.
You'd gotten your degree
and got out of it early on,
and I gotta hand it to you,
you never did go back to
boujyville but stayed as
independent as you could,
creating the first paperback

bookstore in the land, opening
a bunch of doors so that worlds
of peoples could realize San
Francisco as one of the most
priceless cities on the planet,
still a city small town like a
kid at a window somewhere
dreamed of way back when.
And of course got into trouble
with the law after you published
Ginsberg's *Howl*, becoming
activist poet-publisher in defense
of language, your own poetic
voice with its lilting whine of
a drawl, distinctive in its way,
memorable and therefore imitable.
Ah, *fratello*, you should have
been at those many tables in
Vesuvio's, Specs, and the Caffe
Trieste when your poet-biographer
Neeli Cherkovski had us all
doubling over, as you would
have also, at his almost perfect,
always slightly envious but ever
affectionate impersonation of you.
Because you already were a legend
by the '70s, encircled by a transparent
but unbreakable wall of image with
a capital "I," which only Jack and
Allen otherwise possessed. Populist
in poem, paint, and motion, you
critiqued my work for being too
arcane and esoteric, while you stole
from all the poets you loved, giving
their phrases new contexts. A master
husker of American corn, ironic
deconstructivist of the rhythms of
patriotic cliché, you had a dream
and would not go gentle into that

war-zone. Even after I joined the
CLP in 1980 and you'd be chuckling
calling me black Jack Stalinski, till
the S.U. fell under the U.S. threats
a decade later *e l'Italia cominciava*
ad entrare nelle nostre vite fisicamente
e poeticamente, we kept that synharmonic
glyph of friendship intact through the
editions of Artaud, the death of my
son David, your Populist Manifesto,
eruptions of Central American poetry
that the Roque Dalton Cultural Brigade
translated, which you published for that
ongoing cause of liberation. If there were
any brushes between us, they were paint.

2.

These later years, this millennial decade
when we've become closer out of brotherly
need in a time of great anti-semitism against
salaam alekem as well; and with Allen gone,
who was a light—and also I imagine a heavy
—cargo for you, we know there's no God
to judge or forgive us, there's only this singing
to life what comes from the human immensity
of Death. And that's why, putting into the
computer file of the Revolutionary Poets
Brigade Anthology, "At Sea," the finest poem
you've ever written—and you wrote it this
very year, at the age of 90! —I have a sense
of the greatness of the victory over Time and
Despair an authentically true poetry embodies.
So write-on, young timer, you who opposed
the wars in Vietnam, the Gulf, the invasions
of Iraq and Afghanistan. Write on, first-baseman
in your ninth decade, with legs still able to give
my vodka-leaden ones a run for the bases.
"Well, sure, because I ride my bicycle every

chance I get." To see you a few days ago in
your Francisco St. flat after a bout with Staph
Infection, who drilled you one in your heart-socket
when they were fitting a pacemaker in, though the
antibiotics make you tired your complexion's still
rosy, and I know all you wanna do is get up and
go downstairs and drive to your China Basin
studio where alone you never are. So, chorus-sure,
we'll give you one more standing O, big guy.
Chorus-sure, let's sing the "Bella Ciao," son of
Carlo Ferlinghetti di Brescia, and Clemence
Albertine Mendes-Monsanto, your Sephardic
Jewish mother. Together they gave you your
mouth and fitted you with some terrific genes,
and prophesied: Pacemaker, pacemaker, or no
pacemaker at all. Our boy will live till the raven
turns white. *Auguri!* Lawrence Ferlinghetti, *Auguri!*

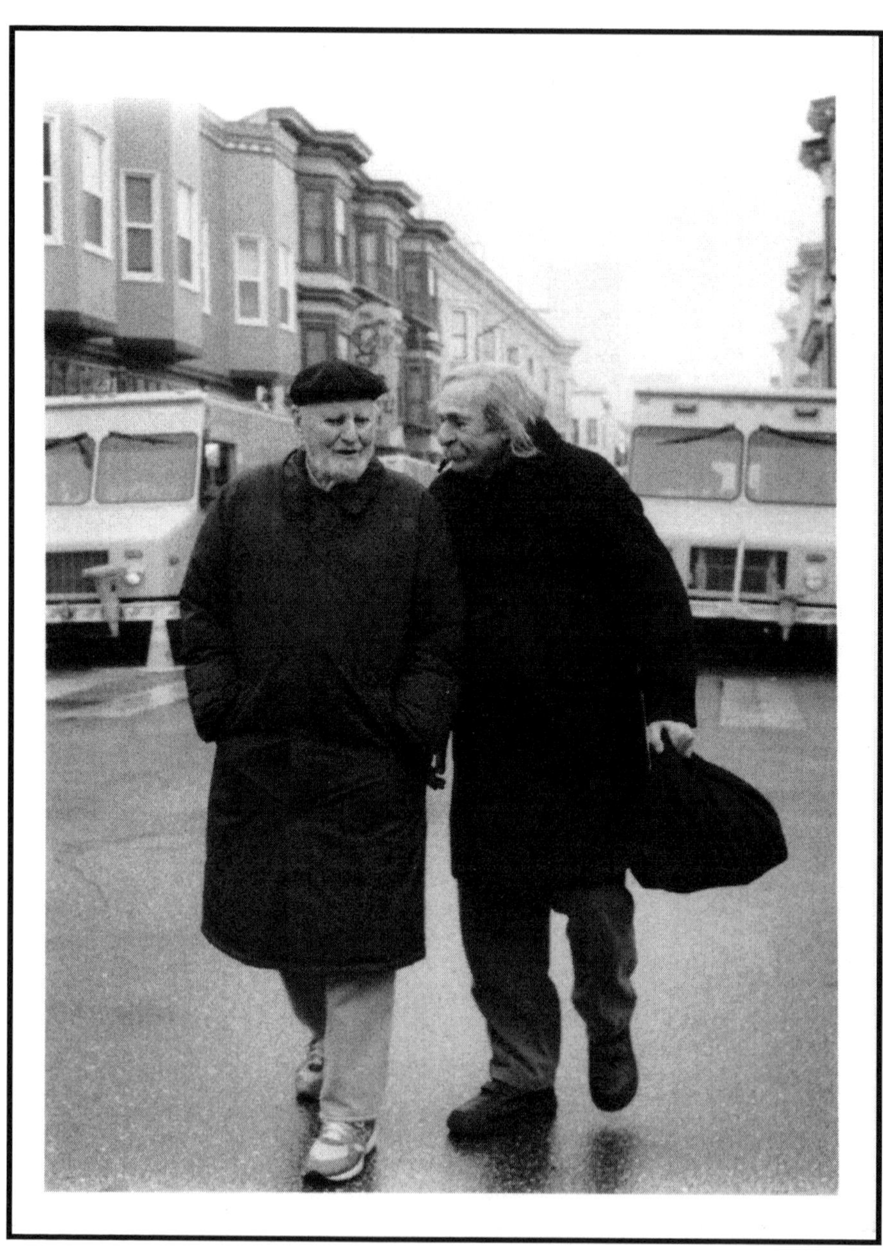

Lawrence Ferlinghetti and Jack Hirschman **John Perino**
Grant Avenue, San Francisco, 2011

Blue Eyes

Agneta Falk

What blue eyes you have!
The color of an infinite sea
Or a sky raised from all
Corners of the world,
The better to see the light
Strewn all over the streets,
Words lifted out of a brush
With big, hearty strokes
        and
Many times around your
Kitchen table, our spoons
In bowls of bonhomie
And poesy, hearing your
Chuckles at the absurdity
Of it all, as you entered
The hall of fame with
A humility and grace
That still echo within us all,
Whether it comes from
Your brushstrokes
Or your pen.

And let the light come through
the inner light of the canvas
the inner light of the models posed
in the life study
the inner light of everyone

"Instructions to Painters & Poets"—Ferlinghetti

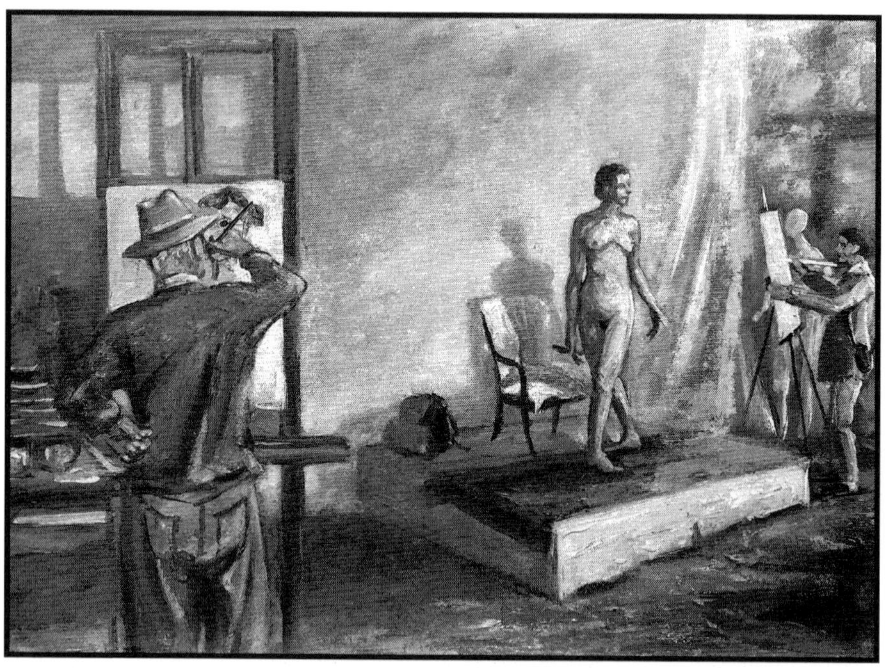

Lawrence in his Studio I **Anthony Holdsworth**
18" x 24" oil on canvas, 2012

Lawrence invited me to attend his weekly drawing group at his studio in Hunters Point. I attended for several months. I began, like everyone else, drawing the model, but after several sessions, I became more interested in observing Lawrence's interaction with the model.—A.H.

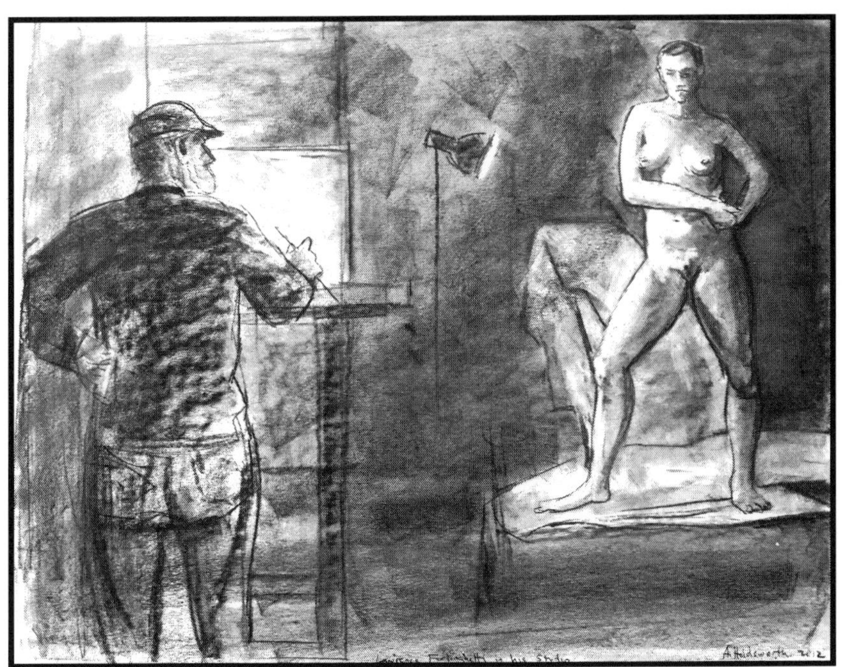

Lawrence in his Studio II & III **Anthony Holdsworth**
18" x 24" compressed charcoal (II) / charcoal and ink (III) on paper, 2012

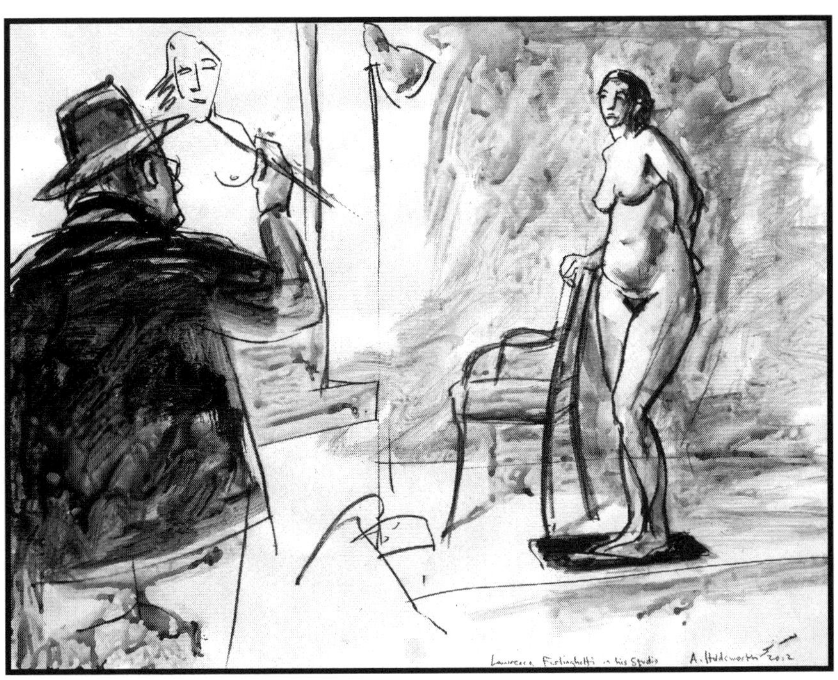

Lawrence at My Desk

Bobby Coleman

after "Allen on My Bed" by Ferlinghetti, which accompanied an exhibition of his art at the Sonoma Valley Museum of Art, 2012

Lawrence is with me
here at my desk
an art bomb
more powerful than Nagasaki
and when I see his face
I know the truth of the experience
and the love that prompts the peace
the terrible sadness of injustice
and the reason he comes here
to show his big sweet yellow of life
a passionate sweetness
not just innocence but a powerful
Veni, Vidi, Vivace
rare yet universal
fluxating from Sephardic heavens
clear across his olive-oiled paradise
a stateless yet ever stately
blue radiance
glowing across seascape eyes
his open door abandoning all despair
and his palette and canvas
the writer and the image
have the same urgency
(a wide-open romance with humanity)
and from the gone and eternal
and from the book of signs
art busts in
bursts our infinite personal colors
into collective arms of joy
stretching upward to the light

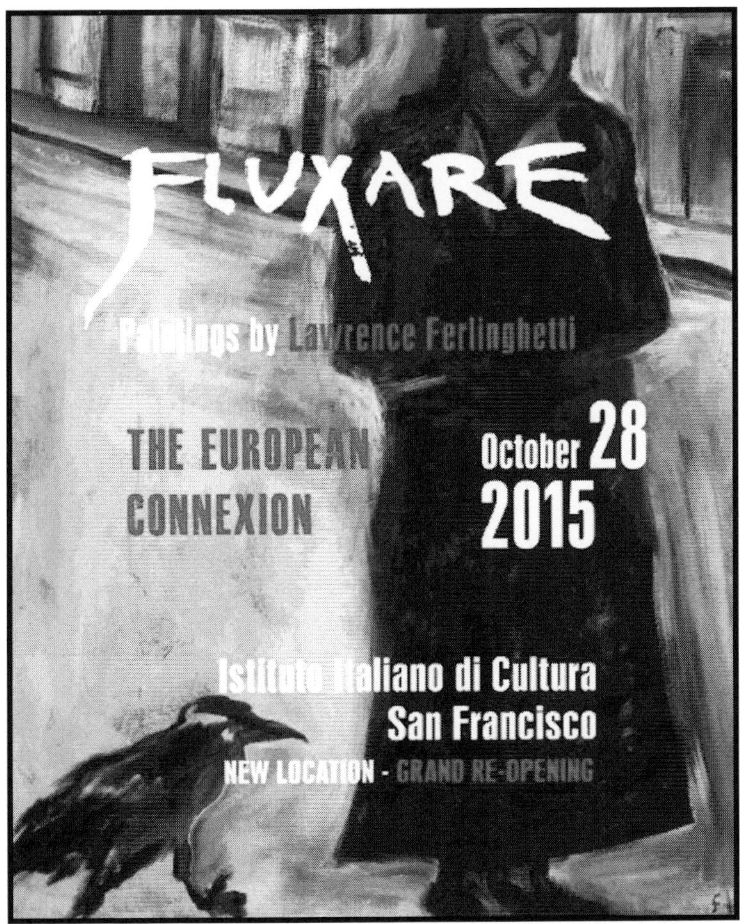

Fluxare Poster **Piero Roccasalvo Rub**
Mother Russia (painting, 1991) by Lawrence Ferlinghetti

Lawrence was invited to officially reopen the Italian Cultural Center's new location with a dedicated exhibition that I curated, *FLUXARE—The European Connexion.* He absolutely loved the poster at first sight, called it "the best ever," and then kept it at the entrance area of his house. On the opening night, he shared the story of his creating in Verona the new Italian verb *Fluxare,* meaning "to love without touching," referencing the Fluxus art movement. Wishing everyone to fulfill their own dreams and to live one's life to its fullest, he conjugated the verb in Italian, making the full house laugh and enjoy a truly unforgettable evening. **Mauro Aprile Zanetti**

Lawrence Ferlinghetti—a Recipe for Life

Mauro Aprile Zanetti

A painter before a writer and a poet, a publisher and activist who took part in some of the twentieth century's toughest social battles and wars, Lawrence Ferlinghetti was always at the forefront of fighting for minorities and human rights, all the less fortunate ones in need of raising their voices. He actually started painting back at the end of the 1940s—not by chance his master thesis at Columbia University was about the art critic John Ruskin's essays on J.M.W. Turner's light in painting—and he never stopped creating art until a few years ago because of his quickly deteriorating eyesight, when he had to finally leave his brushes by the color palette to dry.

Ferlinghetti had seen it all, from surviving the Great Depression as a *little boy*, several international war-theaters such as Pearl Harbor, WWII, Normandy landings, and Nagasaki's atomic aftermath, having served in the Navy for four years and four months with never a job at a desk, always sailing breaker after breaker, the man and the sea. At the end of the 1940s, coming back to the U.S. from Paris, where on the G.I. Bill he had earned his doctoral degree from *la Sorbonne* in comparative literature with a dissertation on the city as a symbol in modern poetry, Ferlinghetti eventually left New York heading far west with his wife Selden Kirby-Smith, looking for the *Last Frontier*. At the dawn of the 1950s he settled in a Mediterranean-like city, where a *San Francisco Renaissance* cultural movement was building momentum from poet Kenneth Rexroth's circle.

In 1953 Ferlinghetti joined a fellow intellectual of Italian origin, Peter D. Martin, to create a "literary meeting place" in North Beach, disrupting every other bookstore business model in the U.S.: open until midnight seven days a week, publishing and distributing paperback editions only. This new cultural format—truly a *literary space* of powerful creativity attracting some of the best underground talents from all over the nation as an inspiring incubator of ideas and values—created a new wave of American counterculture which thanks to Allen Ginsberg and Jack Kerouac gave birth to some of the masterpieces of the world-renowned Beat

Generation. Hence the "Bard of North Beach" ended up being the "Godfather of the Beats" and the patron of their experimentations, producing art and poetry, and live sessions of dissent, to the mainstream.

The "People's Poet"—in the words of Nancy J. Peters, president of the City Lights Foundation—never stopped traveling until a few years ago, always trying to get along with even the most exuberant opposing ideologies. Some of these also turned into emblematic battles he was personally involved in, such as the one for "freedom of speech and expression" when he published Allen Ginsberg's *Howl* in1956.

Because Ferlinghetti enjoyed over 101 laps on earth around the sun, I'd love to share the Italian recipe for a good life: *Mangia bene, ridi spesso, ama molto*—Eat well, laugh often, love a lot.

San Francisco, 2021

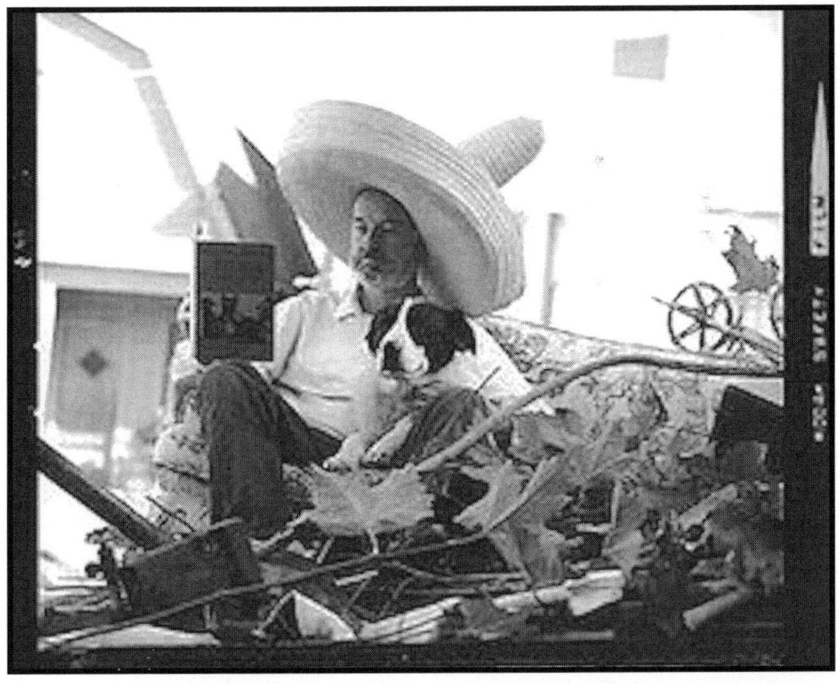

Lawrence Ferlinghetti Reading to his Dog, Homer, in a Dumpster, Potrero Hill, 1970 **Margo Davis**

Words for Ferling

Jack Foley

On his deathbed he asked it:
"Is the nightmare over?"

Not Lawrence—lover of the world.

He remains, in his own words, a poet of *the splendid life of the world*—
a life which is always vanishing.

Is poetry like painting, a visual art? Is it like music, an oral/aural art? Is the poet a public figure, and, if so, what kind of a public figure? How is it possible to create a space for art in a country where art is notoriously devalued (*in two hundred years of freedom / we have invented / the permanent alienation of the subjective / almost every truly creative being / alienated & expatriated / in his own country*)? What is the relationship between books and "the media"? How does one create an audience for poetry? What is the relationship of our ethnic identities to our "American" selves? These are not dead issues but living perplexities, questions which any conscious poet continues to ask at this moment. Lawrence Ferlinghetti's work helps to create a powerful space in which some kind of clarification of these issues may be possible. He remarked at an exhibition of his paintings, *I hope nobody gets the idea that just because it's more institutional . . . that I don't have some subversive intent, or that Eros is at rest.* His vision is of a kind we call "Romantic." But, as Robert Creeley puts it in *Echoes*, the problems the Romantics posited are still with us—we are all "Romantics": "whatsover is 'Rome' is home."

Coney Island
never ends

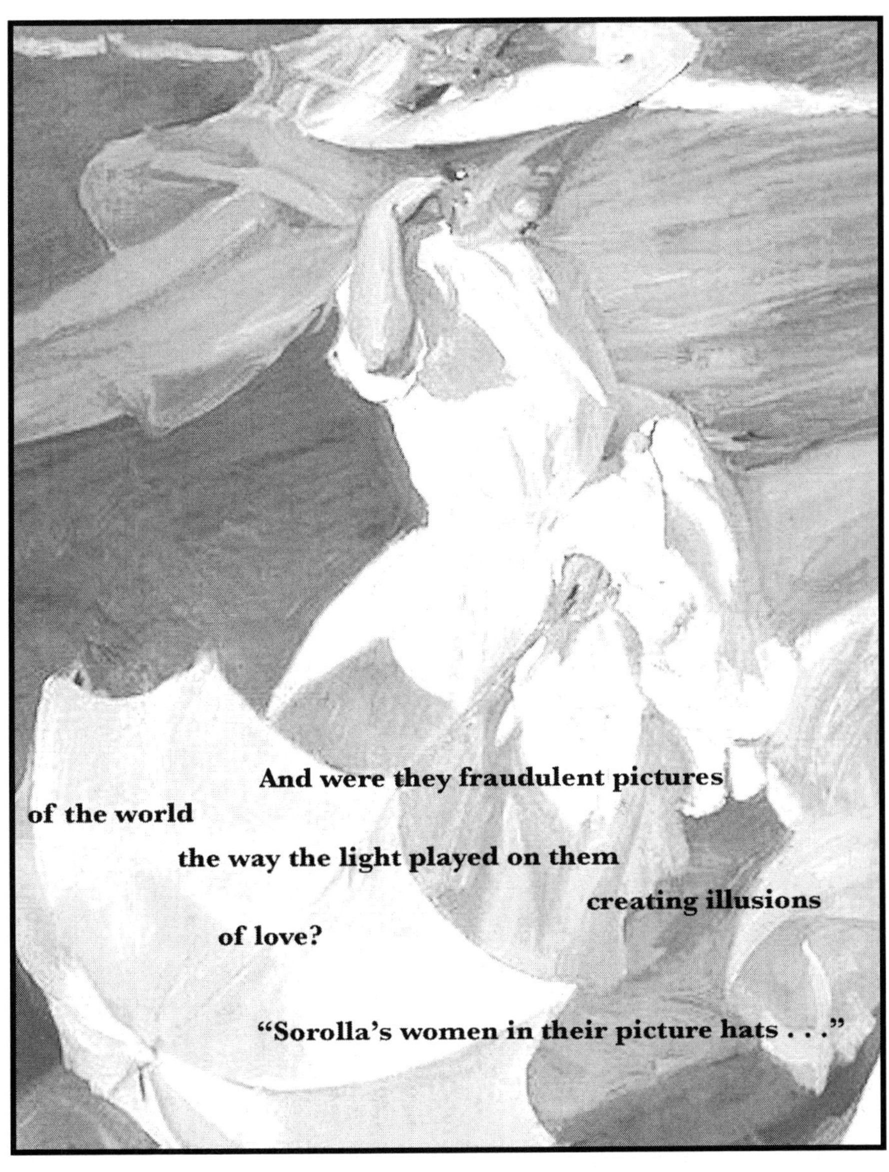

Ferlinghetti's "Sorolla's women in their picture hats . . ." from *Pictures of the Gone World* is based on the art of Joaquín Sorolla y Bastida (Spanish, 1863–1923).

Spotting Ferlinghetti at the Wedding on the Beach

Sara Parrott

after "Sorolla's women in their picture hats . . ."—Ferlinghetti

There's no mistaking the Old Salt
doffing his bowler hat
like a little Charley Chaplin
under the hull of a sun umbrella
near a nest of violins
chasing the basso thrum of the cello
stringing rhythm and guests together.

The bride, a city of white
towering above the tawny dunes,
waits to hitch an arm through his
as he gives her away,
though she never was his

any more than the lighthouse on the jetty,
where the altar of the shore
pushes against the Pacific,
the way his pencil and his paintbrush
trade off,
constantly risking absurdity
on a blank canvas.

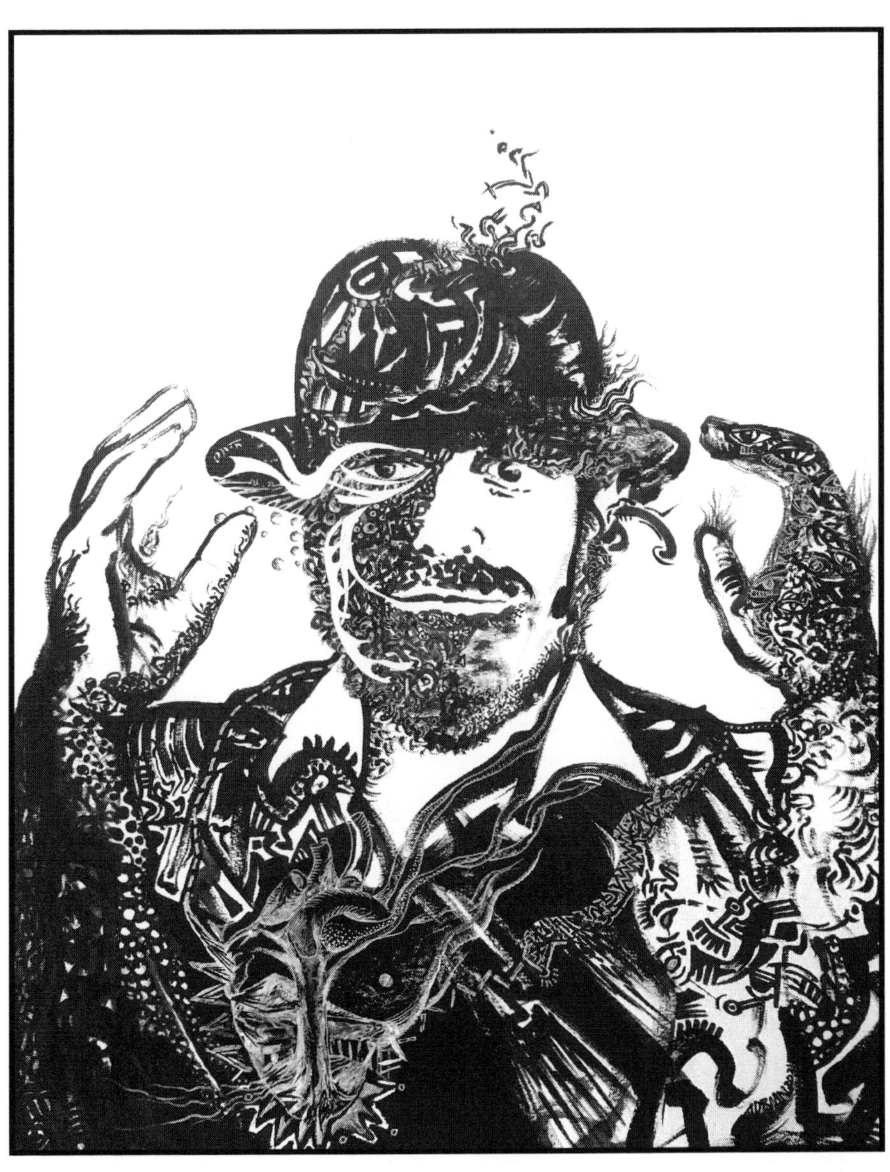

A million in one **Adrian Arias**
18" x 24" mixed media on cardboard, 2020

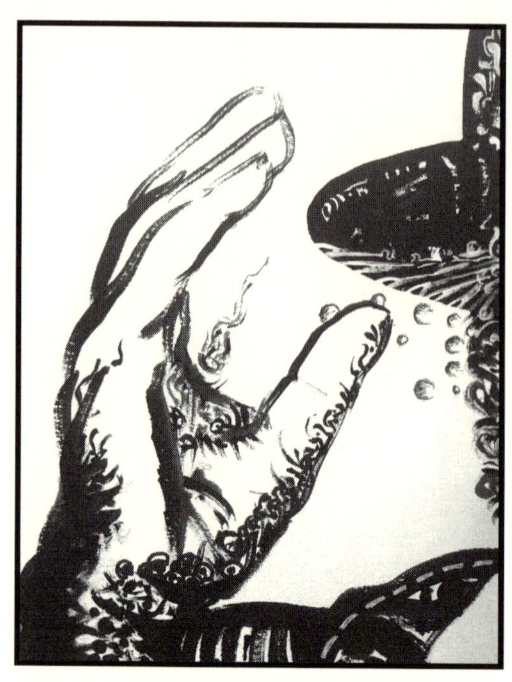

A million in one (details)

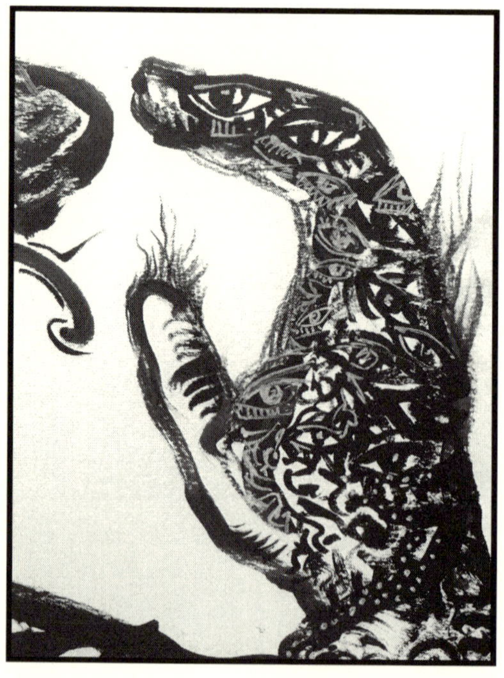

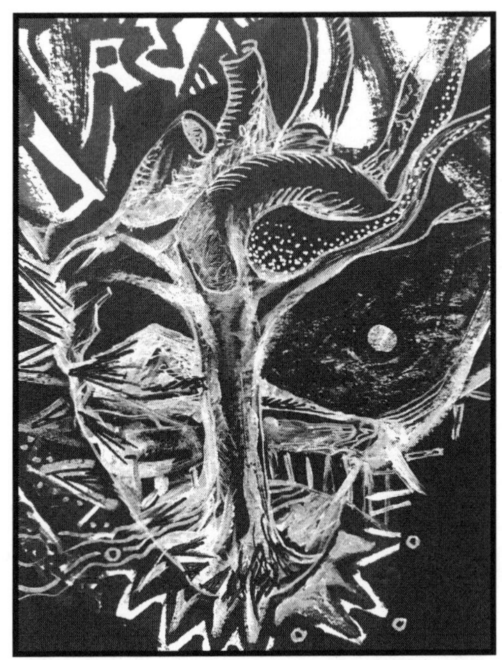

A million in one (details)

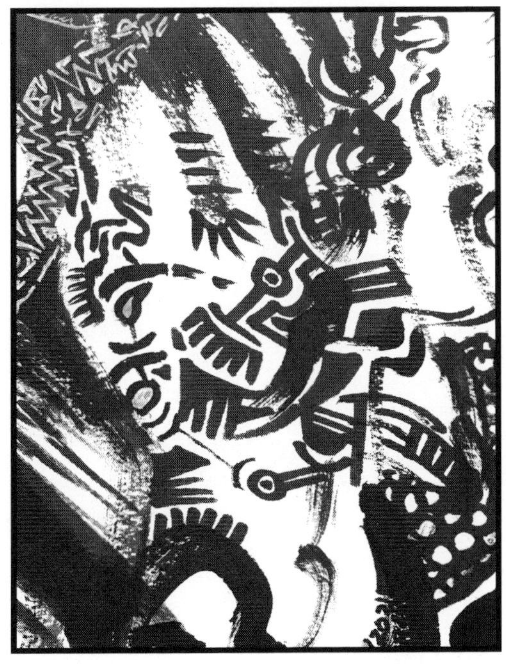

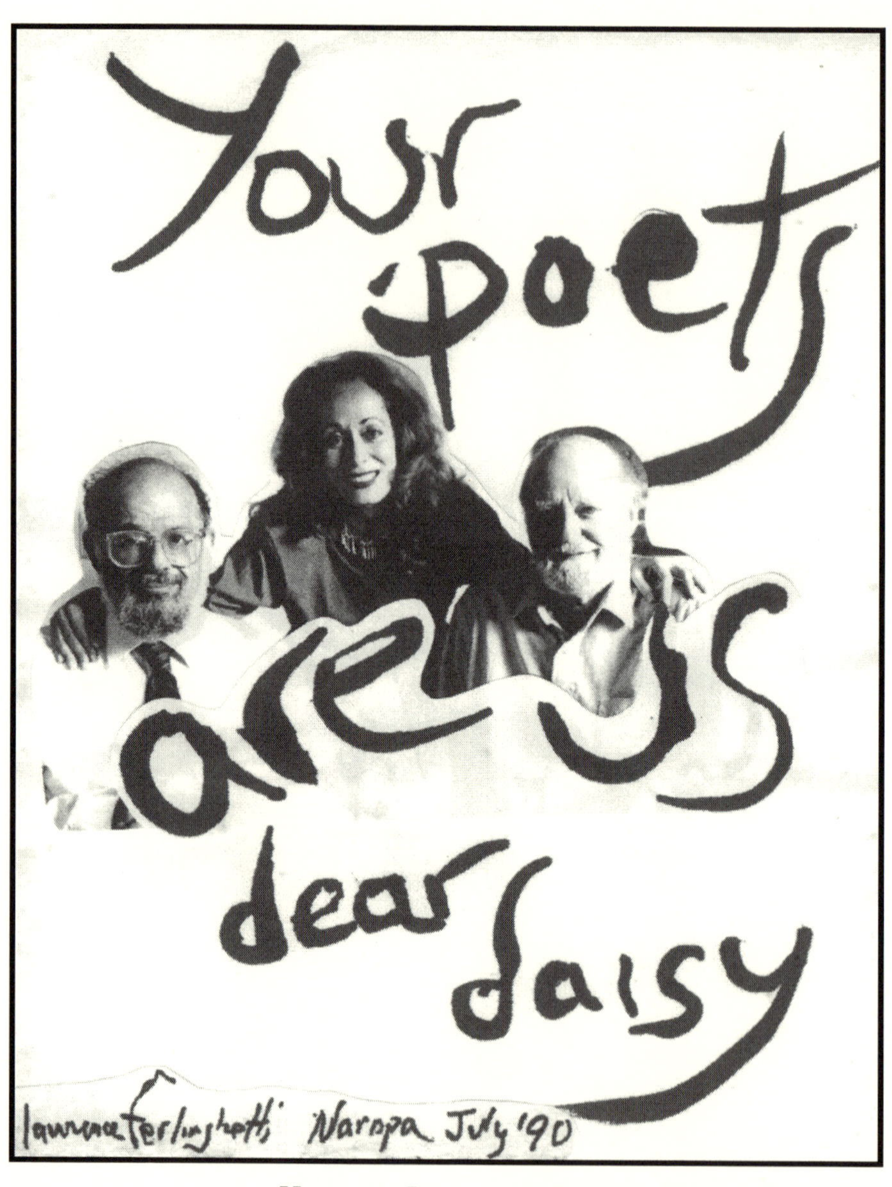

Homage to Lawrence Ferlinghetti **Daisy Zamora**

Epiphany

Cynthia White

I was twenty, breathless
as I climbed the gymnasium stairs
to the poet in the top row
with his hair white as God's
and his long legs
slung over the seat below
and eyes so keen
that all I could do was nod
yes when he offered me wine
from a paper cup and I was revived
and spoke of my love
for his work and would he
sign my book? Before I stood
to go, he kissed my cheek—
a kind of lustful peck—
and ever since I've talked a lot of rot
about benedictions and gifts.
But I'm here to set the record straight.
I kissed him back, and I kissed him
hard. Forty years gone,
I still see stars.

Santa Cruz Poetry Festival, mid-seventies

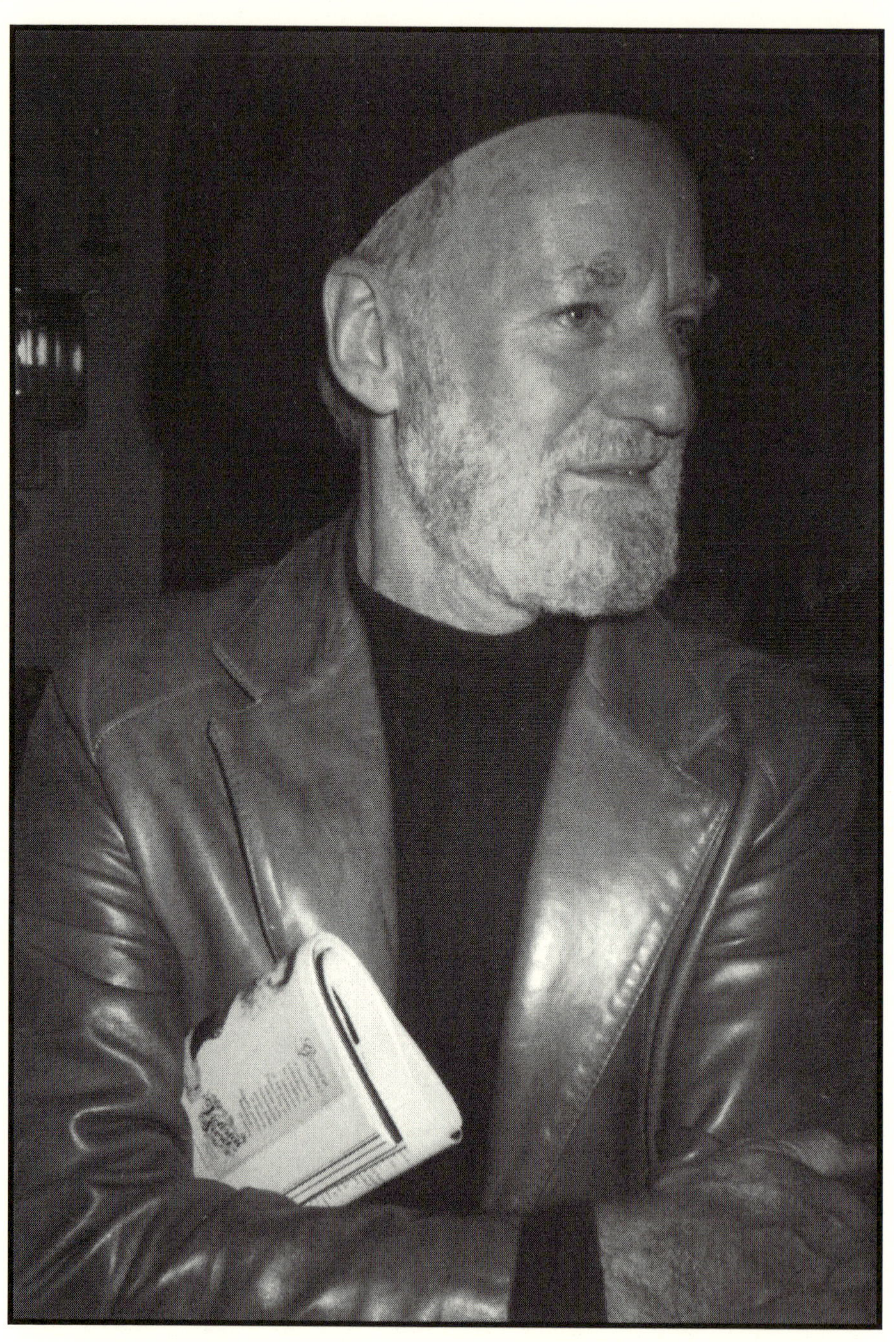

Lawrence Ferlinghetti: visit to New York City, 1981 **Raymond Foye**

Naked Lines
(Hey Ferlinghetti—1998)

Virginia Barrett

> But this past weekend North Beach looked like a theme-park, literally overrun by tourists, and kitsch was king.
>
> What happened to it? What makes for a free poetic life? What destroys the poetry of a city?
>
> Poet Laureate inaugural address, 1998—Ferlinghetti

Hey Ferlinghetti
San Francisco's first Poet Laureate
you know I live in North Beach too—

I see like you each day
        the old Italians
                back on the benches in the park
                        bodies tired but their impassioned talk
        spilling out over the trampled sidewalk
                and often I catch the Green Street Mortuary's
                        marching band as they play
                "Amazing Grace"
        oompah, oompah
        and I have watched the hearse slide by
        driving the photo of the dead one's face

I'm right with you Ferlinghetti
        concerning Fleet Week—those frightening Angels
                and their white cloud streaks
                booming out a sonic screech
in fact I once wrote a poem
        denouncing the planes'
                defacing of the sky

And you know what else Ferlinghetti?
        I had always thought the bridge *was* gold
        given its name
        imagine my shock when I first came
                and discovered instead
                it's painted that fabulous surreal red

I've seen you in the neighborhood
gait erect, eyes straight ahead
and once upstairs at City Lights
you patted Sarah's sweet Catahoula head
and said "She's a word-loving dog"
(with her *own free world to live in*)

I hear you Ferlinghetti—
Poets, come out of your closets,
Open your windows, open your doors,
and YES
I want to dance down from Telegraph Hill
like Lala and Mirabai
singing my naked lines
but you know
it's hard to be heard above all the competing
expressions on the street
the cars   jackhammers   rushing of feet
mostly I end up silently strolling
through North Beach—
Away above a harborful
past the French Italian bakery
the Chinese man selling Van Gogh prints
entering into the park
and the great mélange of people—
drunks Euros Asians yuppies poets freaks
it never differs but changes each week
(we're all a little touched I think
as if sharing something funny)
heading home I linger last
at the flower shop
wishing I had some money

Hey Ferlinghetti
if you ever see me
walking through the neighborhood
I'm usually lost in my own mind space
la vida es sueño real . . .
and this is still a poetic place

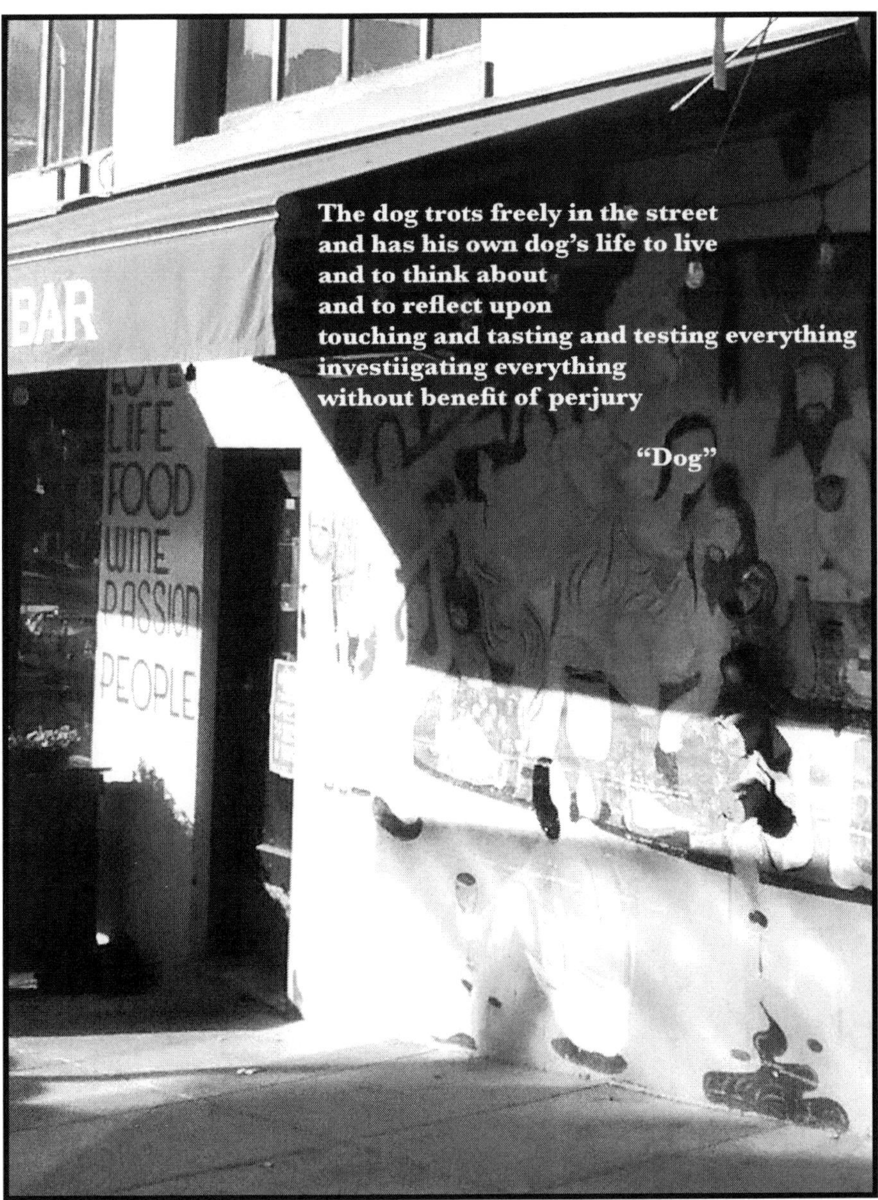
BAR
LIFE
FOOD
WINE
PASSION
PEOPLE
The dog trots freely in the street
and has his own dog's life to live
and to think about
and to reflect upon
touching and tasting and testing everything
investiigating everything
without benefit of perjury
"Dog"

One Morning

Lorraine Walker Williams

> Poetry is the sun streaming down
> in the meshes of morning.
> *What Is Poetry?*—Ferlinghetti

Late September sun warms as I
cross the street to City Lights Bookstore

and climb stairs to the Poetry Room where I
plan to read and maybe buy a book or two,

not prepared to see cameras lining the far wall
and spotlights drowning out sunlight

as the filmmaker greets a white-haired man,
Lawrence Ferlinghetti.

For a poet this is nirvana, so I whisper, "May I stay?"
"If you are very quiet."
I'm barely breathing and promise to be still.

Ferlinghetti first interviews the filmmaker:
Aids Quilt, Harvey Milk, 30 years in the City.

The Poet Laureate of San Francisco begins
his story: *Howl*, Jack Kerouac, the Beat Poets,
admits he was never the poet they were.

Started City Lights in '53, wanted poets
to have a place to speak their work.

He confides: "Awards are meaningless."
Quotes Mailer, "They're like hemorrhoids,
every asshole gets one."

As they break from filming, I approach him,
introduce myself as a writer from Sanibel, Florida.

He remembers the island, we chat,
he signs two books, then returns to muted light.
They've hung a black curtain over the window.

I descend the stairs and step back into the sun
streaming all over North Beach, *streaming down*
in the meshes of morning.

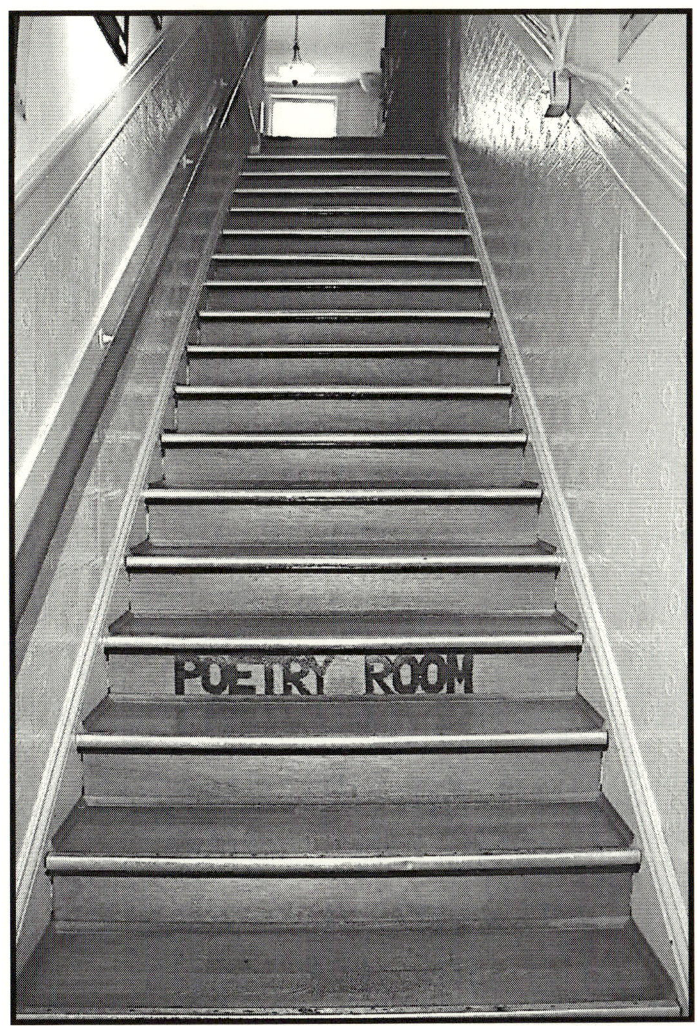

Poetry Room II

Ode to City Lights

Kelliane Parker

On my first visit
I was greeted like a neighbor
In this iconic place of giants

Enters the daughter of a library clerk
My mother taught me to cook, but nourished me with books
Played hide and seek in stacks of LA Main, before the quakes
The perfect backstage pass
For the daughter of a library clerk

Here the books recognized me, remembered me

Me who wooed them to my bed
Caressed their covers, beneath the covers
Pressed my nose near their spine and breathed them in
Writer exposed and waiting
Imploring, "love or want me," and I say, "yes, yes
I need you, need to feel alive again"
I need to feel agony, angry and heartbroken
I want to grieve, seethe and rage
I crave ecstasy, joy and belonging
I want to hold your heavy words and just see them, hear them,
    feel them
I want to taste and smell them, swallow them

The books have not forgotten this kindness, this intimacy
This mercy

I wander through rows and rows
Running finger along titles
Speak their names aloud
And they seduce me
Make me stop and ask
If they want to go back to my place
The ones that dangle the perfectly heartbreaking line
That sharp, aphrodisiac edge that always leads to something

Literature loved being lightly stroked with fingertips
Non-Fiction liked being roughly gripped tight
The Novels, Biographies and Art Books all in need
And when we were done
Done and satiated
We moved on, and nod and acknowledge in passing

But the Poetry, ah the Poets
I loved them again and again, aching for the flood of pain-pleasure
As I roll my tongue around their words over and over again
Committing words to memory by cutting into flesh
Then held hostage to my shelves
To relive the delicious sting of the moment
Just rereading down their spine

Poetry Room III

Atop the Spiral Stair

John Law

Digging deep in the dumpster,
some food for the day.
Later on in the park behind a shed,
curled up inside my bag,
imagine what might lie ahead.

First weeks a barrage of sensations—
different images and experiences abound.
Panhandling with a fake English accent,
coins for coffee at Sacred Grounds,
living in an urban wood without a tent
wraiths of city life all around.

As a child short years before,
family traveled often, Pop would detour
around cities despite my strong request
to pierce the smoggy barrier and enter the velour
folds of the ever mysterious urban nest.
He would laugh and say: we'll miss the mess
and arrive on time!

I grew up on the river,
dog, fly rod, and woods all around.
I lived to leave and no friendly palaver
would stay me, to the woodland bound.
Ever so my dreams were of metropolis
and within gleaming cities to be found,
I knew of such things from books.

Books informed my dreams—
travel the punctuation that made
my inner landscape wrought from words seem
to be more real than real and to aid
me with strength for further exploration
of both, and to impel what made
me dream of transformation.

Sci-Fi Heaven was a sanctuary I found
up the narrow steps above the register,
crouched in the corner never a sound
would escape as I read and read and would infer
from forbearance this nook above the round
stair, was mine as long as I wished,
and none would toss me out.

I didn't know the Beats at seventeen,
Bradbury, Lovecraft, R.E. Howard, Burroughs,
        (no not *that* one yet)
were the tellers of tales from whom I would glean
such joy and my sense of adventure keen.
Such authors upon the shelves I found,
not yet knowing this magisterial word haven's
special place and how world-renowned
Ferlinghetti, the fighter of legal and literary fights
was justly lionized, the poet/soldier/patron
who gave us City Lights.

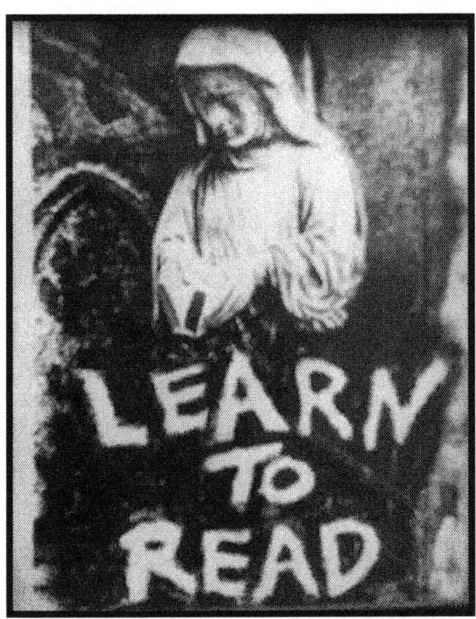

Poetry Room IV

UNDERCOVER
Homelessness Project
City of Poets

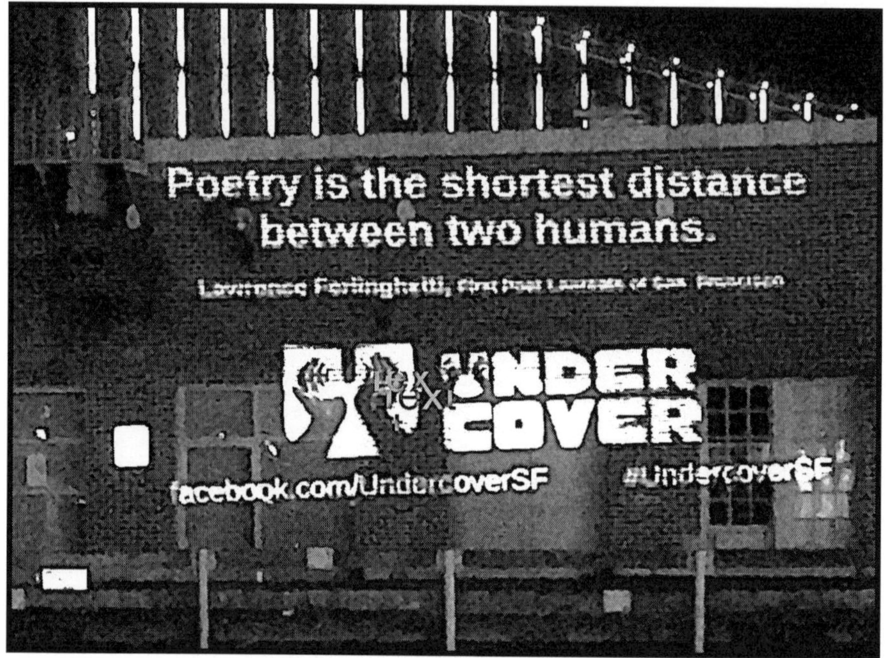

Slogan for a campaign to address the humanitarian crisis surrounding 2016's Super Bowl 50 in San Francisco, which triggered sweeps of the already-suffering population of people experiencing homelessness.

Annice Jacoby

Coming Home from the Bad Poetry Reading

Jane Rades

> We have seen the best minds of our generation
> destroyed by boredom at poetry readings.
> "Populist Manifesto No. 1"—Ferlinghetti

Boring
how can they write such drivel
and then, leaving,
there on the table was Charles Bukowski's
Ham on Rye with a bright yellow cover.
That's telling it like it is,
that's cutting the mustard.

And walking home through Chinatown
the ditchdiggers making an awful racket,
welders, with the sparks flying in the evening dusk,
that's life.

Sparks,
fireworks,
tell it like it is!

Walking home after another reading
where Lawrence Ferlinghetti had read
there was comfort in the dusk.
Things seemed all right
after all of the terrible news on the radio.

No ditchdiggers,
no gravediggers.
World War III,
what are they thinking?

What are poets for, in such an age?
What is the use of poetry?

Elect Lawrence president!
Elect Charles Bukowski vice-president!
Let the poets take charge!

Transmission

Julie Rogers

From some gone world
these wise jewels
spark, catch, and light
at the door of knowing,
nectar & pearls dropped
on the tongue waking
to taste the nimbus
of the poem—wild stars
falling into open hands,
amazements
recognitions
facets with mirrors
where we look into ourselves
as the poet disappears
revealing the heart
absolutely touched.

In this wired culture's
chaos of devices—
the poem misplaced
shelved behind the entertainments
stuffed into cracks between
station breaks, bloodshot eyes
on screens, thought cut short
by texting, the web's weave
silent in somber cafes
where click of keyboards
drowns out gossip, lost
behind the self-help
books—found missing
poetry holds true
beyond spotlights
at the heart of things.

In the long wait to be known
the raw individual

bears a heart starved
for contact, hungry
for some perfect shock
to break the lock off mind's box
where wanting eats us alive—
to find a place
where the naked live
to lie down in a field
of true sounds
gathered like a tribe
of original beings singing
mouths open, holding us
together, leading us
onward into far gone.

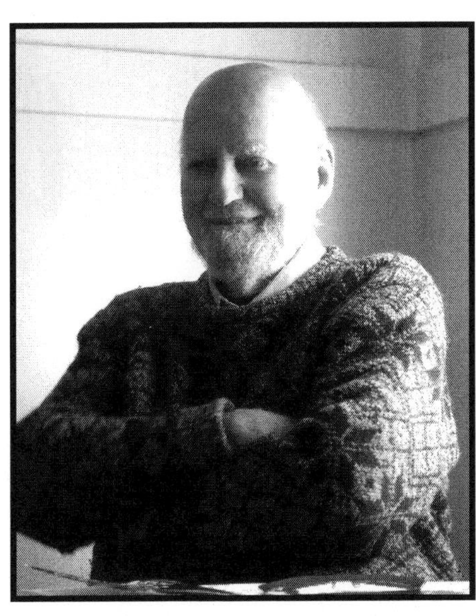

This poem was inspired by a wonderful conversation between David Meltzer and Lawrence Ferlinghetti on January 14, 2013, witnessed at Mr. Ferlinghetti's home in North Beach, SF. Lawrence had just published *Time of Useful Consciousness* (New Directions, 2012), and was then 93—David was 75. I was surprised to find that Lawrence and I held very similar views about "contemporary" poetry. I went home, wrote this poem (in a previous rendition), and it was later published in *Street Warp* (Omerta Publications, 2013). I sent the poem to Lawrence and he graciously wrote me a thank you note.

text & photo / Julie Rogers

The Letter and Syllable

Matt Gonzalez

You brought the poems to us
On your shoulder, leaning against your hip
Occasionally by the shirt collar
Or lying on their cleft-page shields
Some were lunch poems priced a penny each
Others akin to the guttural-canticles
Hearing their be-imaged voices
All the while, in your front pocket
Like a forest grass veiled from daylight
You were saving yours for later
Knowing that every reader asks to be fed impertinences
Yet no yawn exited your mouth
Janitor. Lover. Bricklayer of the word.
Priest. Cyclist. *But not jailer.*
In sense of light-splinter
With a bark-beater in each hand
You scatter-smashed the pulp to make a landing
For the sentence and paragraph
Image and copy, soul-occurred
Codices filled with mouthfuls of silent narrative
Then as now, sister to the in-mostly hurled
Some of those names didn't go away
Ashes charred and scattered, for most
The cranium-hammered
You and a couple of other kids, gray now
A life of blossom-humor
And autumn-protest, well spent
The gone world behind and in front of you
Release the glance-wind
Let your lips find the word once more
This life abhors those who squander
The letter and syllable

from **Forbidden Psalm to the Ram at the Pinnacle of the Mountain**

David Volpendesta

When leaves turn golden
they crumble
in the rough gusts of fall;
do not look at them,
hear them, they come
from a world far away,
visible, but only when
the inner-eye is wide open.

Howling wind and gray boulders
leading to a path that unfolds
to the whistling wind
and the pinnacle of the mountain.
Below in majestic stillness
a man with a white beard
rests his cane on a ledge
and listens to the stars
speaking in slow motion
and sidereal vertigo.

Ah, the breathless beauty
and the wonder of it all.
Let a monarch butterfly
escape from folded hands
and its wings will spread the light
of countless souls illuminating the sky
that forever was and will be
as the Sacred Ram raises its head in spring
as it reaches the top of the mountain
which is as you say Lawrence,
you will live there forever with verses
for your poetry, plays, paining and prose
and your translations from French.

We'll be waiting for you, Lawrence,

with your dog-eared dictionary
where the wind blows in all directions
and the sea is reaching
the summit of the mountain
where your smile is etched
into rock, fire, air, water,
and a mysterious ether
as the pages of your poems
become stained-glass windows
so that we'll always see you in colors
when you open your baby blue eyes
in another galaxy so near but so very far away
from us, so very close and so far away;
ah yes, Lawrence, your poems
are now an ancient singing alphabet . . .

Poet's note: Ferlinghetti was born under the sign of the Ram

Portrait of the Wind

Jim Byron

Soft, warm, yet stone, gemlike—a face chiseled by the continual winds of history's troubled eras, gazing aloof, buried in wonderment. Are those steel-blue eyes wandering over the visage of the moment, the reality before them, or are they simply placed like windows, reflecting the outside world while bearing naked the dreaming, immersed soul behind them?

A hand familiar with the pen's touch-language—a hand storied with the stories, musings, poems, and prose from a man of letters' lifetime. One hundred years of grasping, and the hand remains supple with inspiration, ready to work with the tenacity of a mule to explore another canyon in the wild, invisible gorges of blank paper.

A voice, fiery but stoic, setting ablaze the kindling of authoritarianism's dystopian quasi-civilization. Engaged, utterly rapturous, in the Sisyphean effort of civil protest in the endless influx of contemporary happenings. Raised and rising, a vessel of human plea though darkened calendars of despair. It echoes through the museum chambers of a plethora of minds. Accosting the tenebrosity-empowered evils of the world with pure, radiant, scintillating light.

A mind, shimmering, smoking, excruciatingly hot like a crucible, a cauldron of both civic rage and intimate gentleness, contemplates its next clarion call to Rebellion, the next exclamation for Peace and Justice. Endowing meaningfulness to a shadowy and chaotic world, it extols the haunted masses for their strength in suffering being haunted. Projecting, through language, a poltergeist of itself, to assuage the pain of the hurt and to stoke the righteous ires of those ready to form the next resistance against the next corrupt, heartless spires of powers.

A man, singular in role and influence in this universe, whose name shall not be forgotten by the swelling tides of future generations' minds. Lawrence Ferlinghetti, a treasure to the cosmos of sentience.

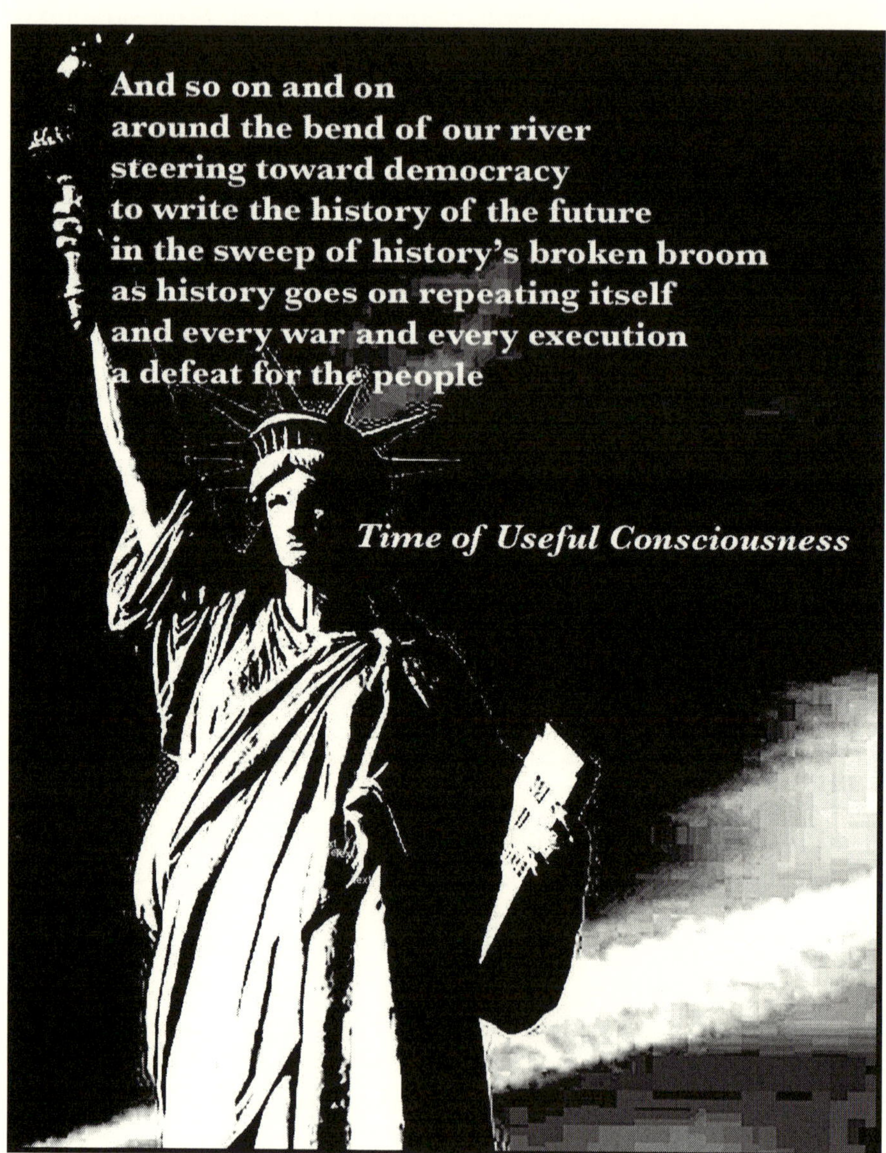
And so on and on
around the bend of our river
steering toward democracy
to write the history of the future
in the sweep of history's broken broom
as history goes on repeating itself
and every war and every execution
a defeat for the people
Time of Useful Consciousness

a grief ago

antoinette nora claypoole

setting:
1968, June 8.
collective heart, beating.
Robert F. Kennedy, funeral day
Nourse Auditorium, San Francisco
"The Incredible Poetry Reading"

one.
los angeles *assassination*
raga. san francisco hippies
welcoming sea cliff gypsies
ancient. delphi oracle reborn
he writes her. prophesied
lyrics. as his own. onyx. eyes
scorn forlorn. vile. country,
stigmata pierces scarred ears,
bleeding, inspiratus. sainted
audience. cannot applaud.
cannot. fathom. socked in.
unclear. *death's dominion*.
cannot relate. confess. one
decade. lost, two. brothers.
on raging righteous television
lips. he dares. chant. his dirge
translates a scantiness of soul.

two.
quiet world watching america
the secret. meaning of things
unnamed. before. we became
soldier's parade, lyrics unafraid
of death. by fear. petroglyphs
written on rampaged nation
tombstone. raga incantation

remains.

eternal.

three.
in this, life. we define
refrains defying rages'
proclaimed, shallowed
demise. yes, he. refined
slain. Trevi innocence
fountained lost wishes
tossed inside reverent
barricades of lost roses

on a page
in a poem
at a reading
the american
the italian
the bay
his. love
her. misty
kiss. before

a grief ago. he was.
naming indigo muses
as confusion. adorned
illusion, unearthed he
invokes nasturtiums
on cliffs of our eyes
his. coins, our Troy.

four.
we travel through his lines, concubines
with his 1968 rhymes disrobing time
we wed his secrets. of things parading
through our festival. of collective regret.

Poet's note:
title/phrase *a grief ago*
credited to Dylan Thomas in Ferlinghetti's poem "Assassination Raga" (1968).

3

Happy 100th, Lawrence!

March 24th, 2019

So like Nanao
                    in my old age
   I'll be a strange wild
                wandering old man

Back Roads to Far Places—Ferlinghetti

Lawrence Unfurling

Indran Amirthanayagam

Let us go down to San Francisco. Let us go down
in March, on the twenty fourth. Let us tell Lawrence,
thank you for that Coney Island of the night fantastic,
for publishing the best mind of his generation howling
despite censors, police, legal obscenities. Let us say,

thank you for all the translations, from Spanish, French,
Chinese, British. Thank you for the lights, the sign
on your office window. Open door it says. Open
heart. Open mind. What would we be if we had not read
your pocket poets with the neat black and white borders?

Where would our nation, our world, walk, hand in hand,
black and white, gay and straight, if we did not have
you saying come out, come in. You are one hundred.
We have become one not only on the ferris wheels,
not only in bar mitzvahs, at the altar, in the baptismal

font. We have become one, not only walking together,
arms locked, behind the coffin of the hero cut down
before her time. Our time is now. You help us understand
these freedoms we share. Lawrence Ferlinghetti, American
and World Poet. Friend. Reporter in the field after

the battle, picking up corpses, preparing for their burial,
and sowing the land again for the next hundred, thousand,
million, billion stars in the night sky. Where shall
we go next? To what distant new home, Lawrence?
Have you got a poem in pocket, ready for the ride?

En el circo del alma

a Lawrence Ferlinghetti en su centésimo año

Rafael Jesús González

Su luz era de las luces de la ciudad,
las luces de la isla de coney que le hacían
trucos, algunos de maravilla, en su mente.
Dejó la manzana grande para vagar y buscar
una dorada y vino al estado dorado
para encontrarla en la puerta dorada donde el poeta-
pintor-ratón de biblioteca creció sus alas y apadrinó
una generación con ritmo de jazz, cansada y fuera
de ritmo con una América presumida y cruel en su temor
de no ser lo bastante grande, holgazanes en busca
de beatitud zen en el camino al fin de las tierras
donde no pudieron mas que volver el gañido en aullido
que el poeta-pintor-proveedor de palabras difundió
a un EE. UU. de A. mojigato y defendió su derecho
de ser escuchado ampliamente, el aullido que llamó al oeste
una generación más jipi contra una cultura propensa
a la muerte a comenzar una revolución de amor y goce bastante
para ponerle el alto a una guerra imposible. Y a la vez en el circo
del alma, corazón grande pero no holgazán nuestro funambulista
larryferli cortejó a la desafiadora de la gravedad
belleza ciega que más veces que no
arrebató a medio vuelo porque le dio visión.

In the Circus of the Soul

for Lawrence Ferlinghetti on his 100th year

Rafael Jesús González

His light was that of city lights,
the coney island lights that played
tricks, some wondrous, on his mind.
He left the big apple to wonder & to seek
a golden one & came to the golden state
to find it by the golden gate where the poet-
painter-bookworm grew his wings & godfathered
a generation with a jazz beat, beat tired & out
of beat with an America smug & cruel in its fear
of not being great enough, bums in search of zen
beatitude on the road to the land's end
where they could not but turn the yawp into a howl
that the poet-painter-purveyor of words broadcast
to a prude U.S. of A. & defended its right
to be heard wide, the howl that called west
a hippier generation to counter a culture bent
on death and start a revolution of love & joy enough
to stop a hopeless war. And all along, in the circus
of the soul, big hearted but no bum, our tight-rope-
walking larryferli man courted gravity-defying
blind beauty that, more often than not,
he caught in midflight because he gave her sight.

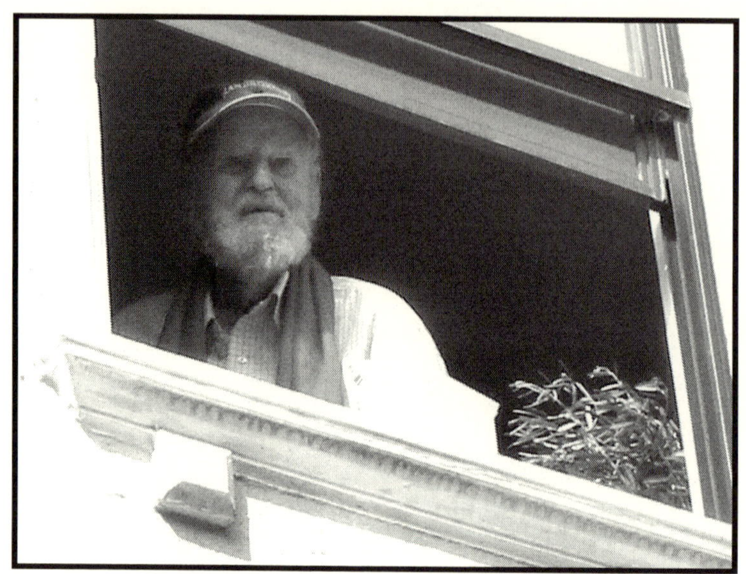

On his 100th birthday, San Francisco's Conspiracy of Beards—a 30-member male choir who perform *a cappella* arrangements of Leonard Cohen songs—serenaded Lawrence under his window at home. A surprise arranged by his friend, poet and painter Agneta Falk, the event took place in the morning before the big celebration at City Lights. After three verses from *What is Poetry?* the Beards sang "Happy Birthday" and one of Lawrences's favorites, "Take Me Out to the Ballgame." He listened from his window wearing a red scarf, which he waved in playful appreciation.

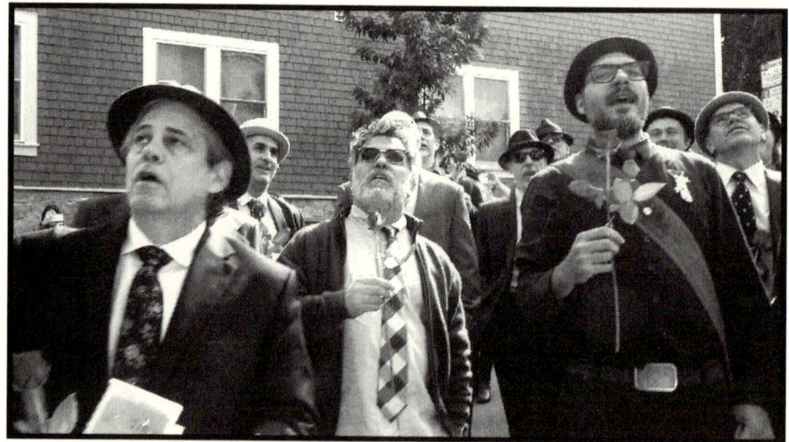

Lawrence in his Window as the Beards Serenade **Lou Dematteis**

A Century Is Something Else

Alejandro Murguía

For Lorenzo on his 100th

When the skeletal ruins of Nagasaki popped
their wasted eyes on the shore of eternity
and death raised a skinny rose in honor
the Poet stood there to witness the crime
as it should be

When in Spoleto the words of the ancient bard E Pound
floated like leaves in a pond
and signs were everywhere that poetry lived
in the aching pulse of the human heart
the Poet noted that scene with tears
and it was hip

When Poet told story of journey with Ginsberg at his side
along the spine of Nuestra América
To riff with Neruda thus uniting with poetry
the continent South-North
it was so cool

When subway poets, misfit artists, forlorn street corner outlaws,
& misunderstood words were cast out by miscreant politicians,
shady cops, & defrocked priests—the Poet threw open the doors
and shouted Come in! Come in!
all you who dig poetry, anarchy, happiness, struggle,
alleys & bars & sunsets
even Coney Island hot dogs fit in a poem
It's all good
It's the paella of life which is poetry
And it was cool—very very cool

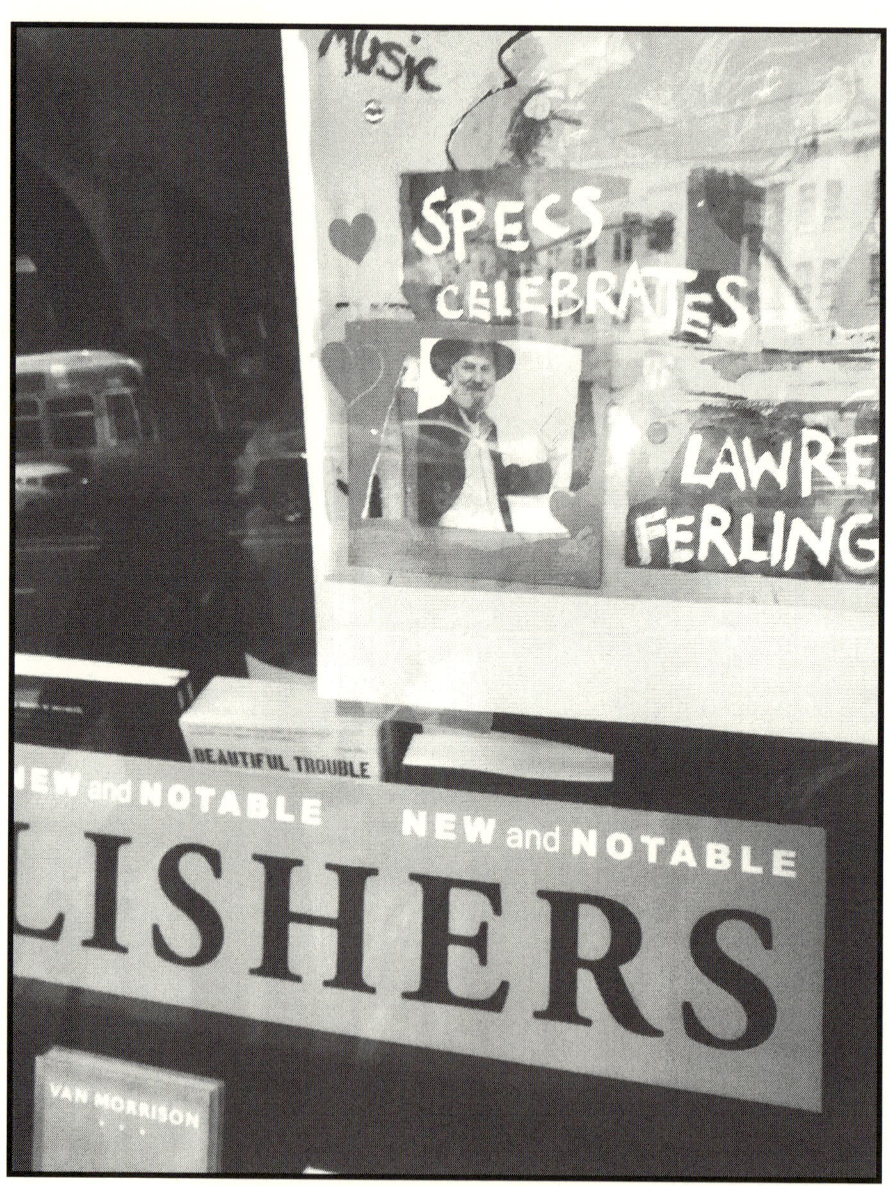

Specs' Twelve Adler Celebrates
North Beach, San Francisco, March 24, 2019

Ferlinghetti Free Association

Richard Ivanhoe

City Lights
Still Delights
Pocket Poet
Can you grow it?

Start in Yonkers
Don't go bonkers;
Then to France
Give life a chance

Tar Heel
Nagasaki
Second reel
Getting rocky

Columbia U.
Sorbonne
North Beach, too

Peter Martin
Pocket book carton
Somethin' new startin'

Marx and Lenin
Brighter, lighter
Lennon-McCartney
I want to be a
Paperback writer

Howl, Growl
Add a vowel,
Don't throw in the towel.

Caffeine routine
Subteen scene
Queen ravine
Not obscene

Clayton Horn
First Amendment
Still lives on

Coney Island
Secret Meaning
Never silent
Progressive leaning

Big Sur
Woodpile Buddha
Facial fur
Red wine and Gouda

Far Rockaway
Of the Heart
Fluxus, Paint with Sunlight
Who are We Now?
Insurgent Art

Useful Consciousness
Blasts, Cries, Laughter
Greet Great Career
Still more after:

Across the Landscape,
Our mouths agape
Poet, Painter, Publisher, Bookseller
Traveler, Translator, prolific fellow

Little Boy,
Still a joy

Poet Laureate
Pacifist anarchist patriot
Political rally
Kerouac Alley
Landmark status
100 years old, still coming at us.

Is there anything else that counts light of our days the morning light early morning light that pours in over the rooftops through the leaves of trees through their lovely branches stretched to the rising sun

Little Boy—Ferlinghetti

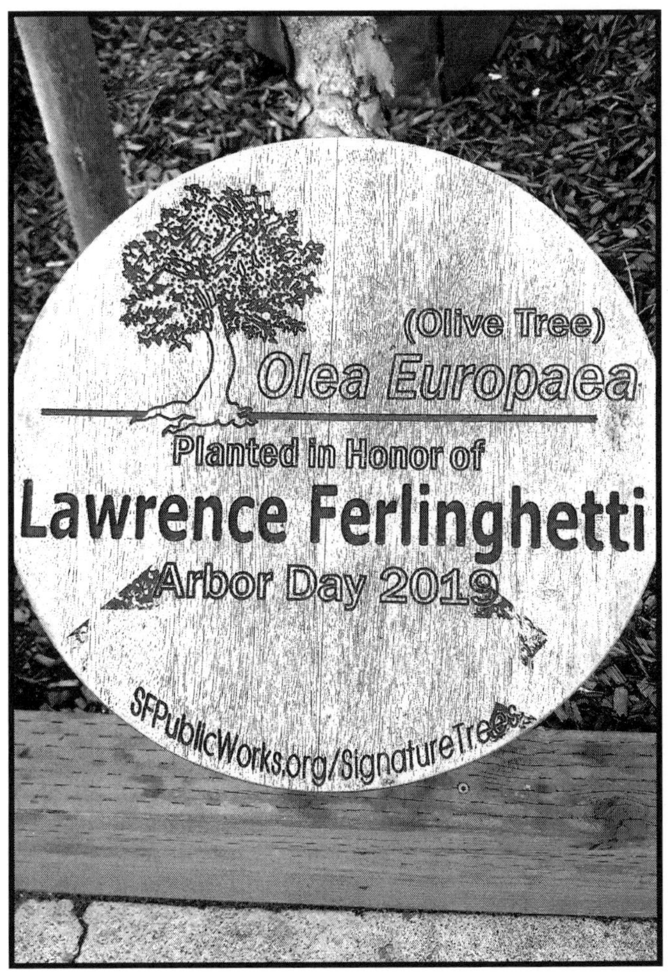

There are readings of his poetry, exhibitions of his paintings, parties, an olive tree planting and more. The San Francisco Mayor's Office is scheduled to announce an annual Lawrence Ferlinghetti Day on his birthday, March 24.

Chloe Veltman, KQED, March 15, 2019

Haiku for Lawrence

Janice Mirikitani

Like the moon rises,
Tyranny cannot stop
poetry lighting the dark.

Happy Birthday, Lawrence. It's been a privilege to know you for over 55 of your 100 years, at GLIDE celebrations, in poetry readings. You have always been a brilliant mentor and source of inspiration for me.

You influenced Rev. Cecil Williams and me as we founded a new GLIDE in 1965: Celebrations (not Sunday religious services) and a myriad of Glide Foundation programs that provided much-needed free meals, recovery circles, coalition building to make noise against dictatorships, war, and injustice/inequity in America.

In 1967, your poetry inspired us to create new liturgy for our Sunday Celebrations, including your poem which we had the community read out loud together: "I Am Waiting…for a Rebirth of Wonder…"

We defined ourselves in all our glorious differences and common humanity:

> "This is the gathering of the tribes.
> Hip, square, straight, deviants, perfumed lace,
> And multi-colored cultures, races,
> Gay, lesbian, trans, bi, drag queens, questioning,
> Whatever gender, religious, non-believer definition,
> Ladies with fur hats, children without shoes,
> Headbanded long haired, shaggy bearded, smooth shaven,
> Unbathed, booted or barefooted.
> Here we open boxes, erase lines of categories,
> Kill assumptions, strip naked our stories,
> Lay bare our addictions, see one another/ourselves,
> no better, no worse, no judgment, no shame.
> The Now calls us—invent, create ourselves anew,
> Walk, slide, skip, dance, dash, glide here together.
> Come. Change is of the essence."

Read at the San Francisco Main Public Library's celebration on March 17, 2019 in advance of Lawrence Ferlinghetti's 100th Birthday.

Four Haiku for Lawrence

On His 100th Birthday

Bob Booker

1.

In Chinatown cafe
The customer shouts
"NO TEA TODAY"

2.

End of the month,
Loading up the U-Haul truck
Before the rent is due again.

3.

In Kerouac Alley,
Grey-bearded man hollers
"That's one of those fucking Lefties"

4.

Another sleepless night;
The sound of garbage trucks
Making the rounds all morning.

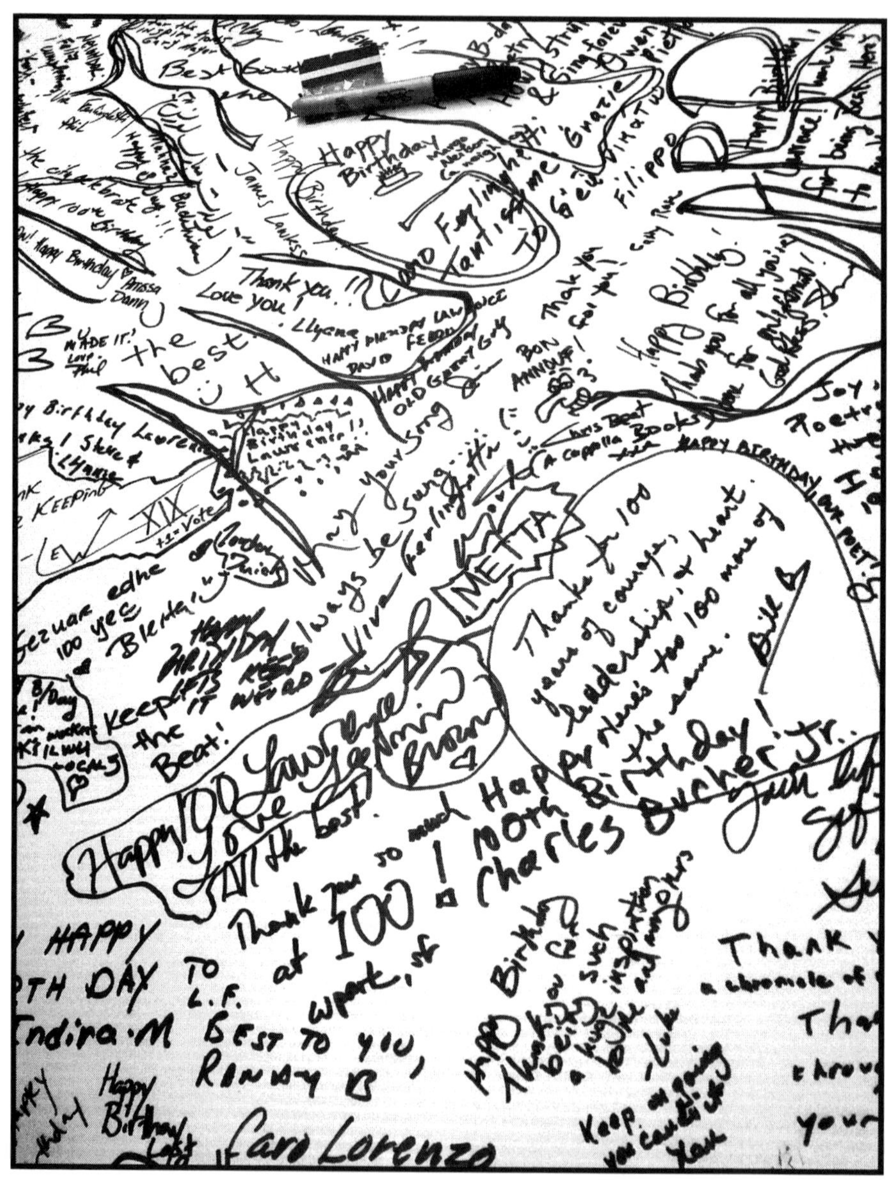

Giant 100th Birthday Card
Jack Kerouac Alley, San Francisco, March 24th, 2019

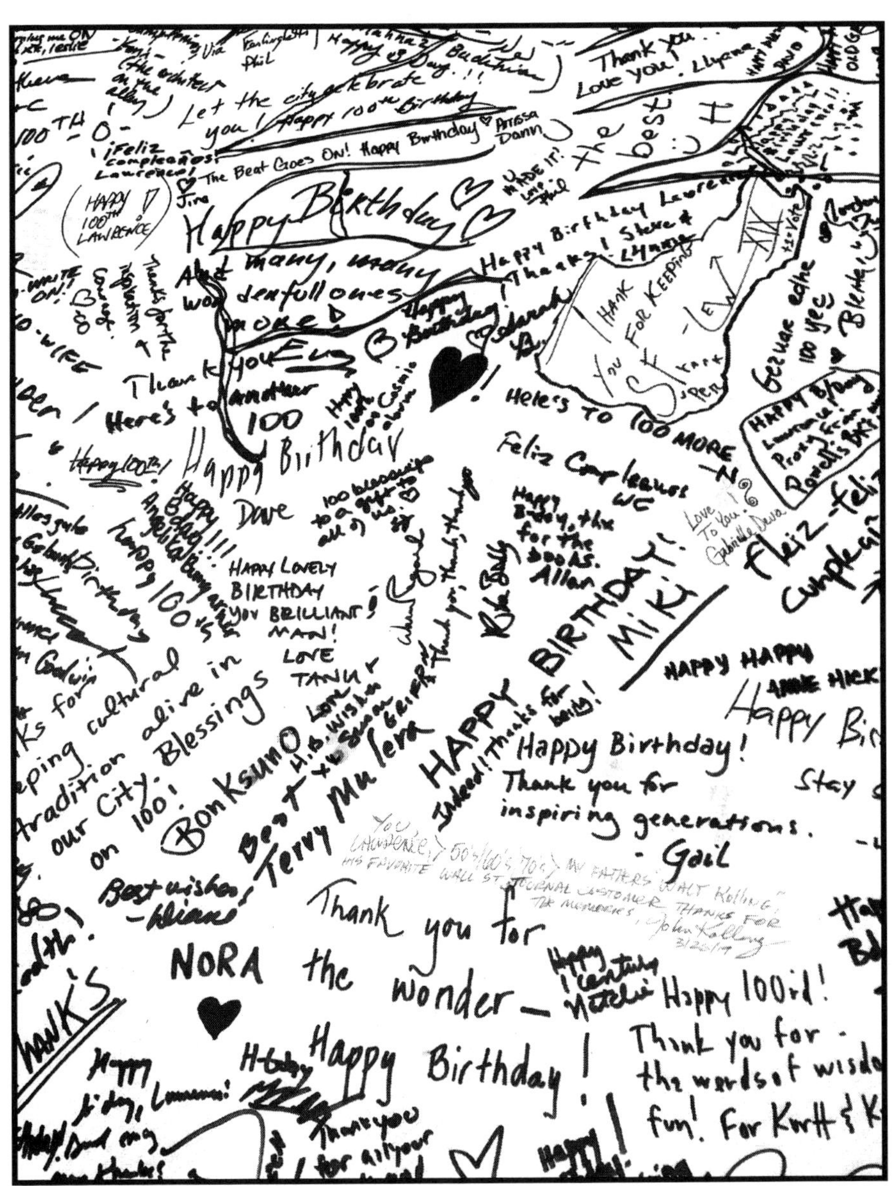

Let the city celebrate you! Happy 100th Birthday
The Beat Goes On! Happy Birthday
Thank you. Love you! Llyana
the best :) H
¡Feliz cumpleaños! Lawrence!
HAPPY 100TH LAWRENCE
Happy Birthday
And many, many wonderfull ones more
Happy Birthday Lawrence
Thank you
Here's to another 100
Here's to 100 MORE
Happy Birthday
Dave
Feliz Cumpleanos
HAPPY LOVELY BIRTHDAY YOU BRILLIANT MAN! LOVE
Love To You. Gabrielle Deva
HAPPY BIRTHDAY MiKi
happy 100's
Keeping cultural tradition alive in our City. Blessings on 100!
Best wishes
Terry
HAPPY BIRTHDAY Indeed! Thanks for being!
Happy Birthday! Thank you for inspiring generations. - Gail
HAPPY HAPPY
Happy Bi
Stay
Thank you for
NORA the wonder
Happy 100i'd!
Think you for the words of wisd fun! For Kurtt & K
Happy Birthday!
Thank you for all your

-Ferlinforus-

c.l. kuckenbaker

Larry-la-la-Lawrence
Tonight is your
NIGHT!
The night of
NIGHTS
100yrs your
Feet have
Crawled waddled
Run danced walked
The Beat
THIS BEAT
We all Beat4
This night
Lawrence the
Room Vibrates
100 memories
Strong
100 foot falls
Long through 100 true
Years
100 ideas mind beyond
THIS SUNDAY
COMING UPDOWN
Is your Island Day
To UNREST!

03/24/19
Second Story - Vesuvio Cafe

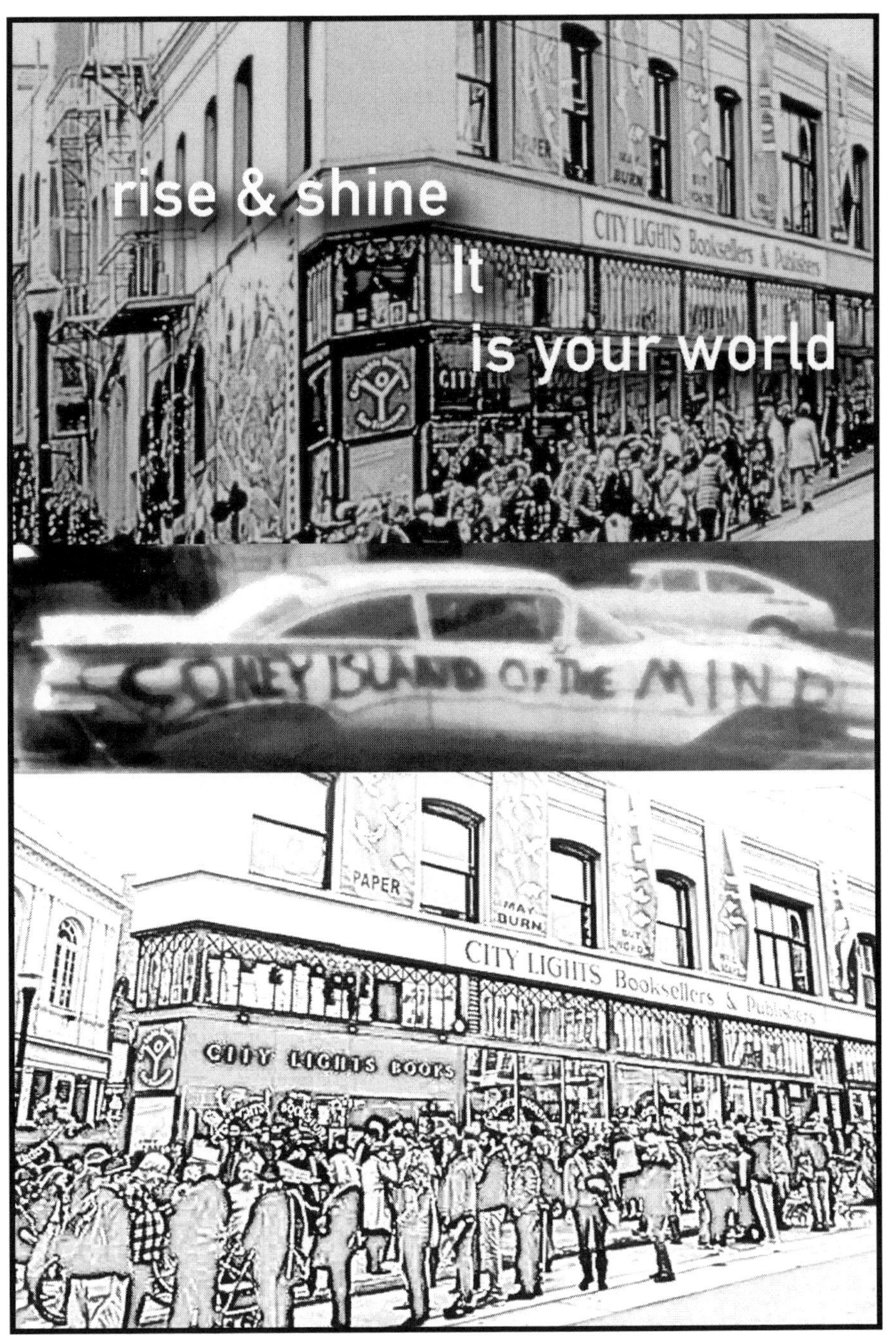

Birthday Crowds, City Lights

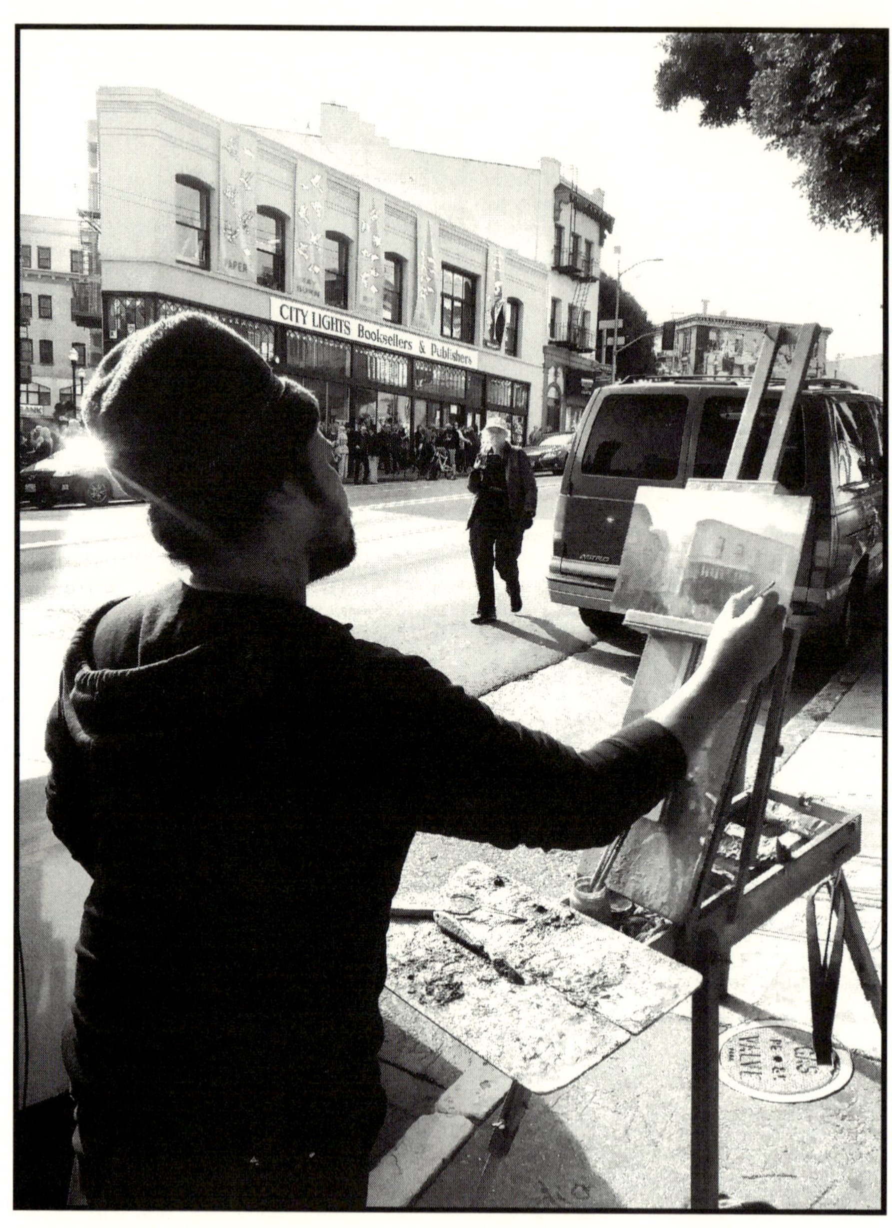

Artist on the Street **Virginia Barrett**

San Francisco Bay Area artist John Paul Marcelo painting City Lights during the 100th birthday party celebration, March 24, 2019.

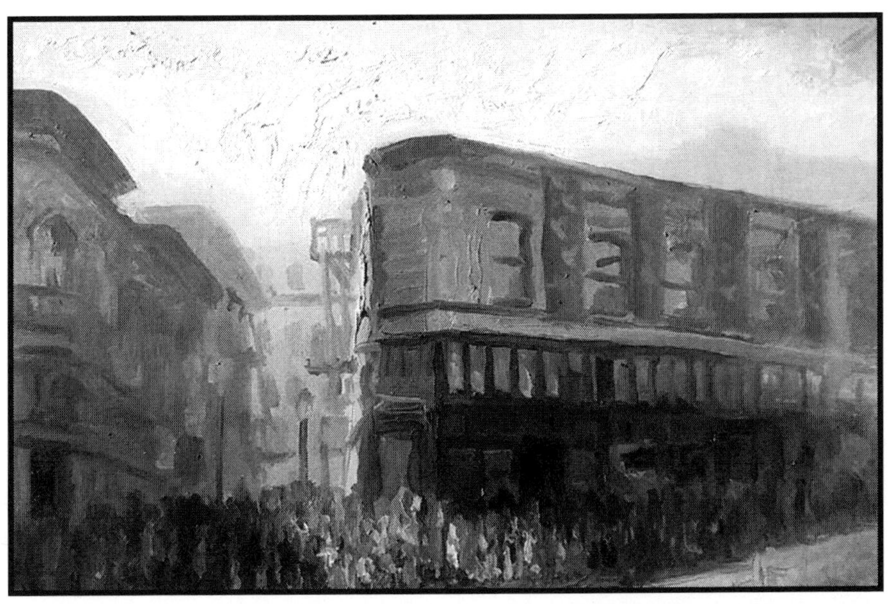

Lawrence Ferlinghetti, 100 Years **John Paul Marcelo**
12" x 8" oil on wood, 2019

And as he took in with hungry eyes the panorama of the City, he saw as never before the panorama of his own life stretched before him, with its unknowable possibilities . . .

Time of Useful Consciousness, VIII—Ferlinghetti

Marina Safeway, San Francisco
March 25, 2019

Karen Poppy

for Armistead Maupin, now in London

Pigeons congregate in an empty parking space,
Spilling over the lines. I stand for a moment as
Seagulls upset the still with their flight and cry,
Swirl the air gray. Then I go in, and no, not to
Whitman, not to Lorca, nor even Allen Ginsberg.
I hope to find Michael Tolliver traipsing through
The aisles with Mary Ann Singleton—any of them—
The Barbary Lane beloveds. Still naive and new.

Yesterday, my 43rd birthday, Lawrence Ferlinghetti's
100th. Everyone mobbed Columbus Avenue, City Lights,
Like those parking lot pigeons, spilling over the lines,
Listening to poetry, words that fed a great generation.
The Beats. I'm sentimental about eras I didn't live in.

In Marina Safeway, back in the day, before tech
Millionaires, before the impending influx of more,
Before Mylar balloons now on display that choke
Our birds, our Bay, before San Francisco changed over,
I'd have roller-skated my way between high pyramids
Of avocados and bananas—myself high—not waiting
For their ripeness, not asking their cost, or mine.
Woken up blissful with anyone, not fearing death.

That Angel had not yet arrived here, unrolling a river,
Merciless and vast, on which you saw all your friends
Float by: wasted to bones, so young and afraid, dying
One after another. Beautiful, then gone. Just gone.
Whitman, Lorca, these are your dead, your children.

Do not turn from them. The Bay is wider than a river.
Is that optimism or sorrow, America lost even then?
As we look forward, look back, was San Francisco?

Trick Meditation

Kim Shuck

Time is a trick meditation
A curved wire
Hammered into not straight
I have put my back to a mast
Let eyes wander right out to their limit
Curious wind direction stories
Offered up

Even today the
Whitefade
Convolutions
Crossing loops of hammered wire
Still curving

Pacific cannot be laid out in a line
New way of reading current and wind
A line of knots
A net to be passed through a hand
A calendar
A hammered wire
Come around to another hook
Another curiosity
Feeds or
Sinks past the barb
Another crossing
Another year
The vanishing point
The next knot

error in time 2

devorah major

Time a traveler
melting
in eternity
(the mind coming and going)
Back Roads to Far Places—Ferlinghetti

time
exists only
as a contract we keep
or break

a memory we smell or forget
a terror we confront or duck
a bridge we blow up
or build

i had been wrong in thinking
time moved
when it was the earth that shook
the sky that rushed
we who surged

i had been wrong
in believing that times changed
when it was the world that changed
as we nourished or devoured
the life around us

not in time
not on time
not despite time
but always
in the moments named now

Tuscan woman with olive eyes
(the whites milk white)
catches the last sun in them
and flashes back the light
"Canti Toscani"—Ferlinghetti

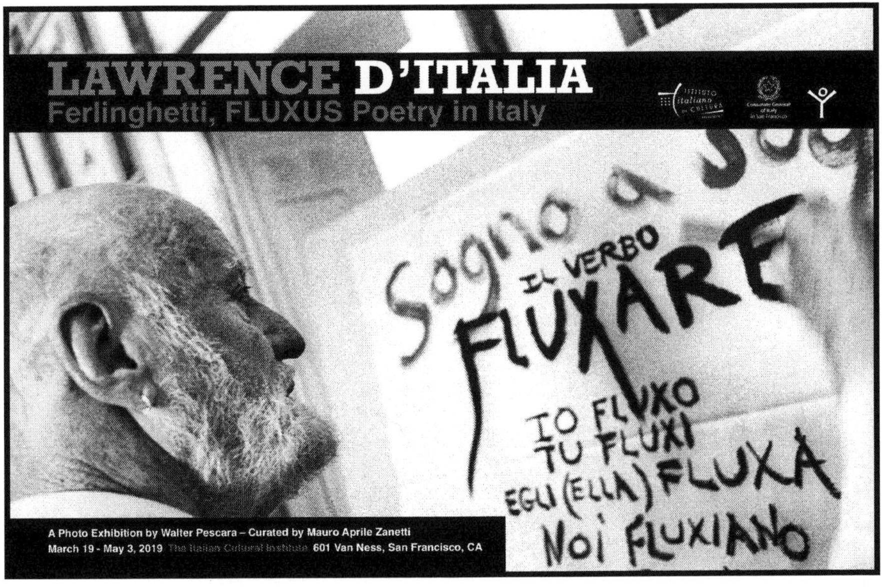

Fluxus, Exhibition Poster **Piero Roccasalvo Rub**

Istituto Italiano di Cultura / Italian Cultural Institute of San Francisco hosted the show "Lawrence d'Italia" for Ferlinghetti's 100th birthday in 2019, featuring an exhibition of photographs by Walter Pescara curated by Mauro Aprile Zanetti. The photos captured Ferlinghetti while performing FLUXUS poetry during his 2002–2005 travels in Italy. The exhibition included gelatin silver prints plus some pieces imprinted on nautical sails.

Trickle Down Beat

Lynne Barnes

> We have to raise the consciousness; the only way poets can change the world is to raise the consciousness of the general populace.—Ferlinghetti

Before I read Ginsberg, Wakowski, di Prima,
before Rexroth, Patchen,
before Hirschman, Corso, Snyder,
Burroughs, Kesey, or Weiss,
before I read Hettie Jones, Kerouac,
or Ferlinghetti,

I watched Maynard G. Krebs,
that goofy, hippie beatnik,
so loyal to his dweeb friend,
so authentic when compared to him.

Maynard tapped our deep
and secret longings—
like thirteen-year-old me—
for something far out beyond Dobie.
Maynard, *like wow, man,* on TV,
nineteen-fifty-nine.

We gay and lesbian adolescents,
we teens molested by our preacher, our priest,
we exceptional athlete girls with no Title IX,
we *bat* and *bar mitzvah* stars
whose grandparents were exterminated
in the old country,
we Black youth, no voice, no say,
heavy thumb of white supremacy
pressing against us—
we all longed to rise.

Some of us, naïve as boot camp recruits,
scrambled up and over the walls of childhood,
pens drawn like floppy toy swords,
no drill sergeant in sight.

Then, at the dawn of the sixties,
a muddle-headed model
be-bopped onto our TV screens,
a goateed, bongo-playing bohemian,
allergic to work but in love with the work
of Thelonious Monk and Dizzy Gillespie.

We're older now, and now we know
it was really you, dear Ferlinghetti,
allowing us to howl, you
and your City Lights and mindful
Coney Island that exploded our Straightsville,
gifted us this visual, comedic, pop beatnik
who opened our world.

Dear brave, sage, centenarian bard,
our hearts fly to you now like released doves,
from those of us born in the hinterlands,
where Maynard, not Allen, G.,
was the first match struck
in the dark tunnel
of our generation's coming of age.

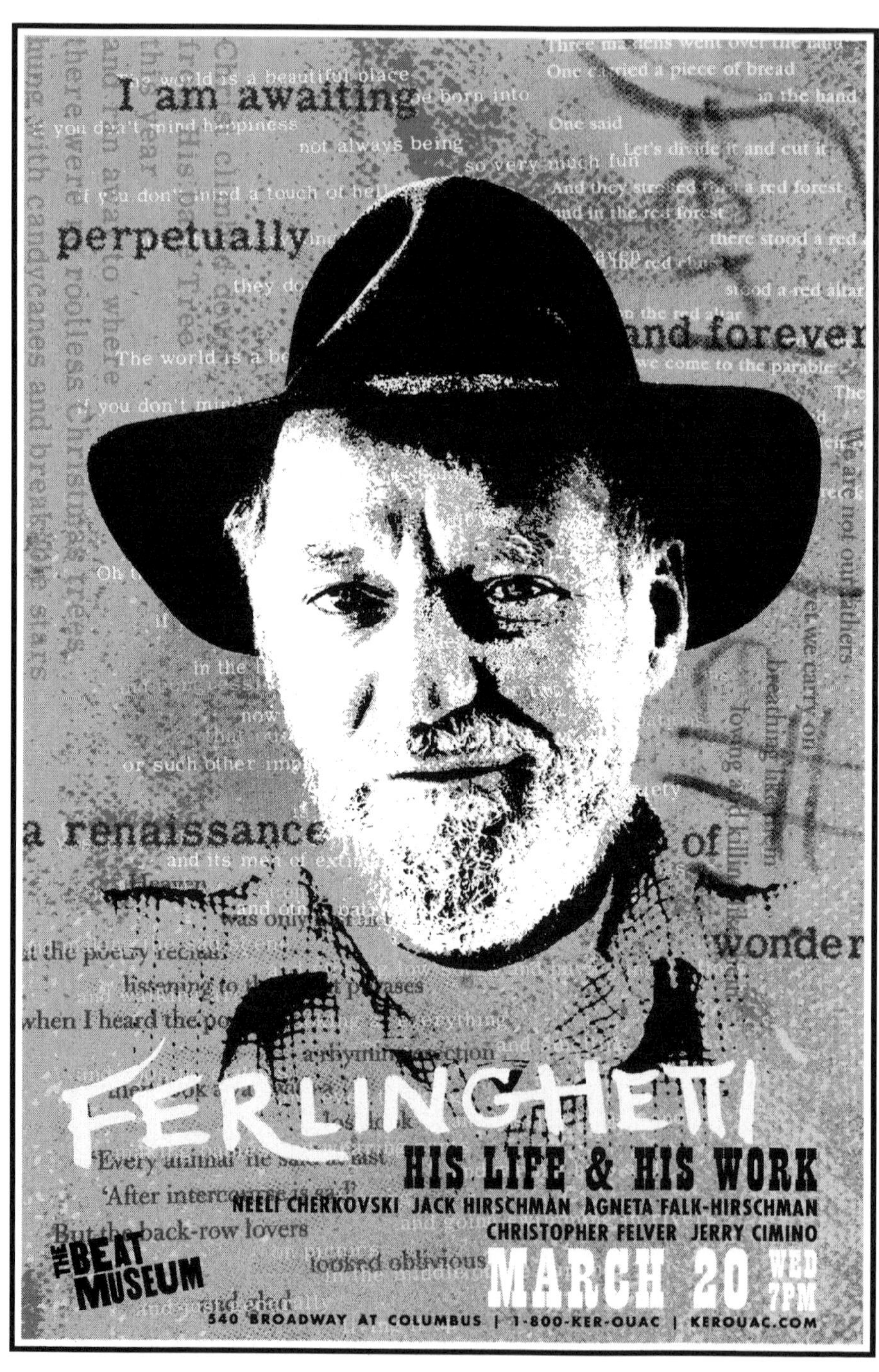

Ferlinghetti: His Life & His Work, Poster **Brandon Loberg**

Keep it 100 and beyond

Rich Stone

A century's worth
Of howling beatific rumblings
A smooth beat to keep
Beyond the pale green light
Of vigilant literary guardians
Illuminating a full-court word-press
Chasing away censorial shadow casters
To the sidelines
Against the oppressive testimonial onslaught
That calls to question
The poet's call to arms
Storming the front
Against a blitzkrieg of fake revelations
Scripted in scrolled ancient parchment
That crumbles in holy unraveling
The poet must float above dead waters
As they boil away below
In an eschaton immanentized
By the fervent presidential spirit
Of Agent Orange Julius Caesar
That attempts to sanctify
The poisoned wells
Of secular futility
In these darkest hours
The poet must pen their light
Against revelatory books of the dead
And scintillate upon the skies
A perpetual glow on those
Who dare encroach
Upon the transparent literary passage
Of our sacred offerings
We will prevail as we must
In spite of an empire's setting sun
Bringing forth a new moon
Where the poet rips away the muzzle
And howls through the darkness of the night

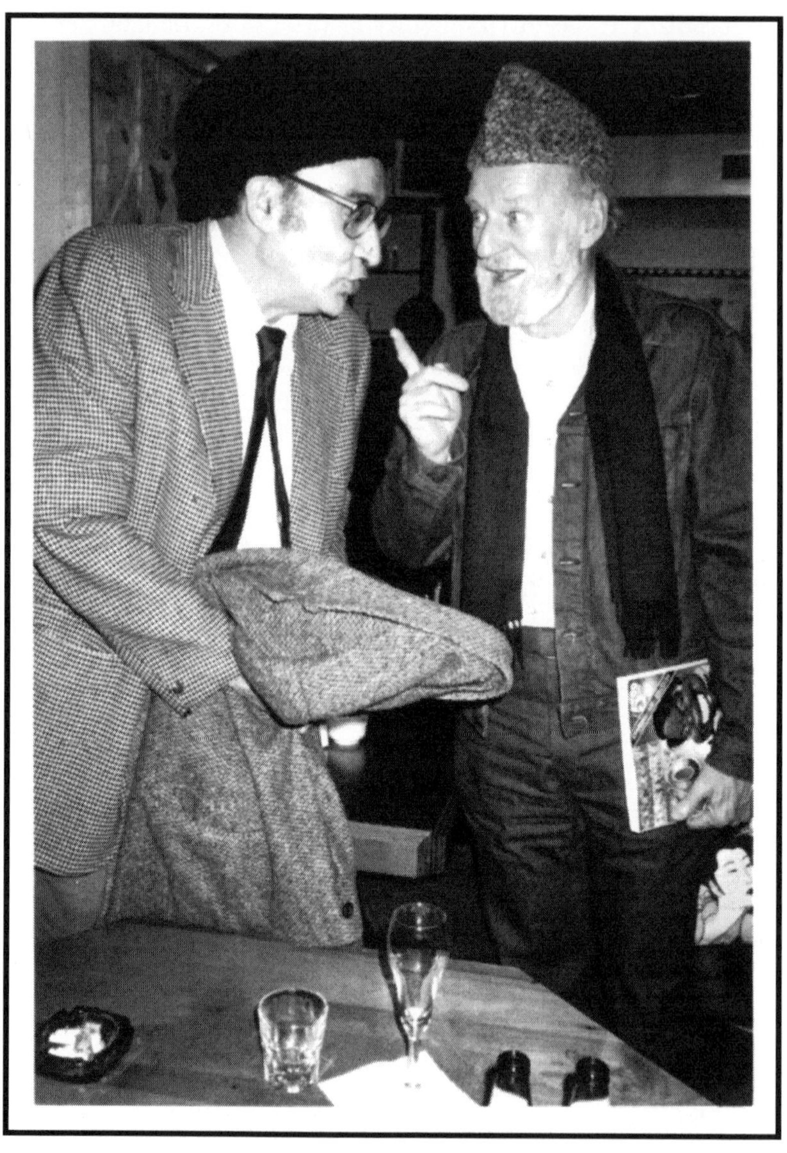

Lawrence Ferlinghetti and Carl Soloman **Raymond Foye**
One University Place, New York City, 1981

Ferlinghetti published Allen Ginsberg's *Howl and Other Poems* (City Lights Books) in 1956. The landmark obscenity trial that ensued resulted in a victorious defense of U.S. free speech and freedom of artistic expression, with hugely positive consequences for the maturation of American culture. Ginsberg dedicated the title poem of the book to Carl Solomon, his friend and fellow writer.

Holy time in eternity holy eternity in time holy the clock in space
"Howl"—Allen Ginsberg

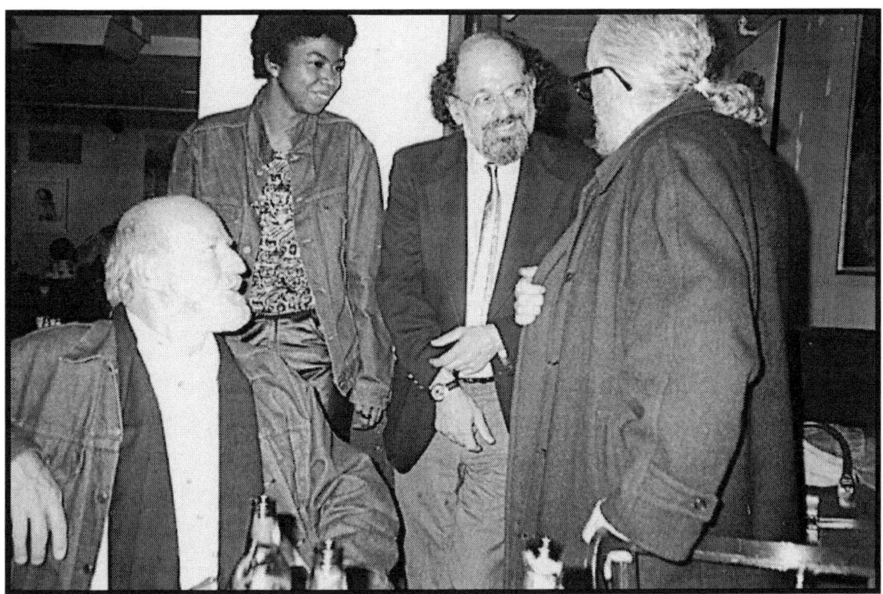

Lawrence, Sheila (Johnson) Carr, Allen Ginsberg, Harry Smith

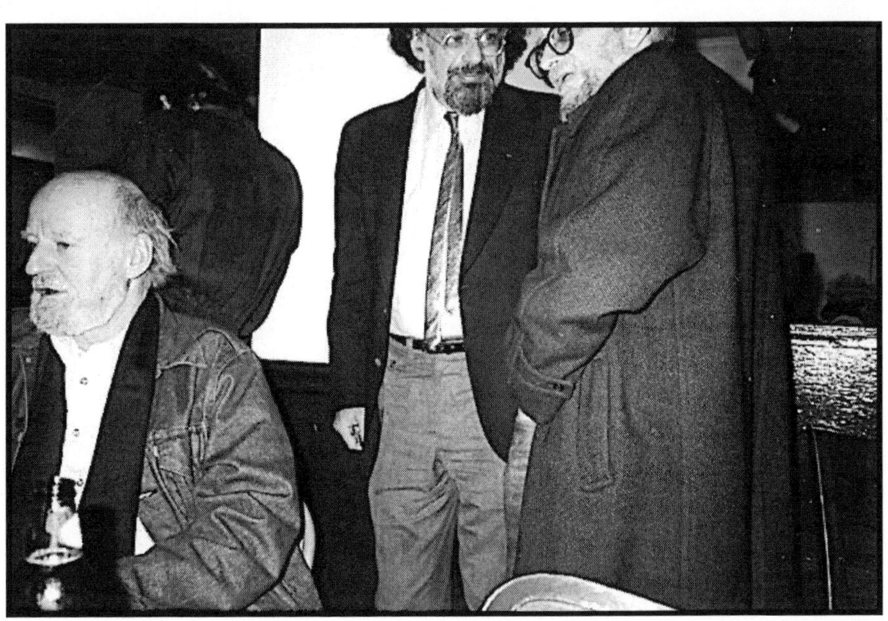

Lawrence, Allen Ginsberg, Harry Smith **Raymond Foye**
One University Place, New York City, 1981

For Lawrence
Upon a Century

D.S. Black

As long as wonders exist in our world
Lawrence Monsanto Ferlinghetti
once masked as
Lady Liberty—inscribed in
the pantheon
of
picaresque American rebels
may signal us *through the flames*

born the same year as folk hero Zorro
his sword a palette plain language
cuts away lies and cant
over all the obscene boundaries

now attains an even century
aren't poets supposed to die young?
beyond simple longevity
one imagines or yearns for
actuarial turmoil
at Lloyd's of London
should others follow suit

Ferlinghetti poet of hope
whose City Lights is beacon and
bulwark against constrained speech
Howl freed from the obscenity of
arrest with clear eyes no longer may
imagination be enchained

His greatness transcends
any notion of nation
at home in the wideness of world
wild lines on long skinny pages collect into books

a library of insurgency

The state of the world calls out for poetry to save it.
Poetry as Insurgent Art—Ferlinghetti

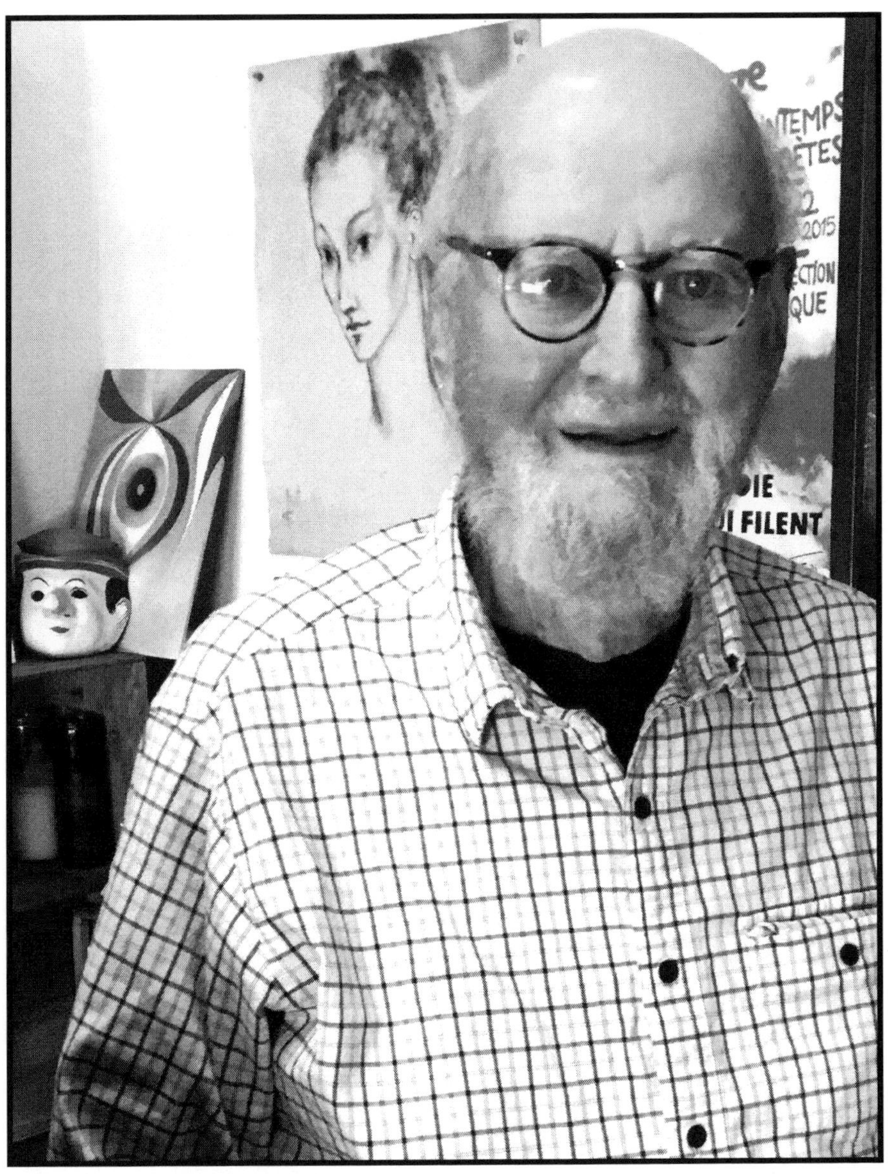

Lawrence in his Apartment I **D.S. Black**
San Francisco, October 12, 2016

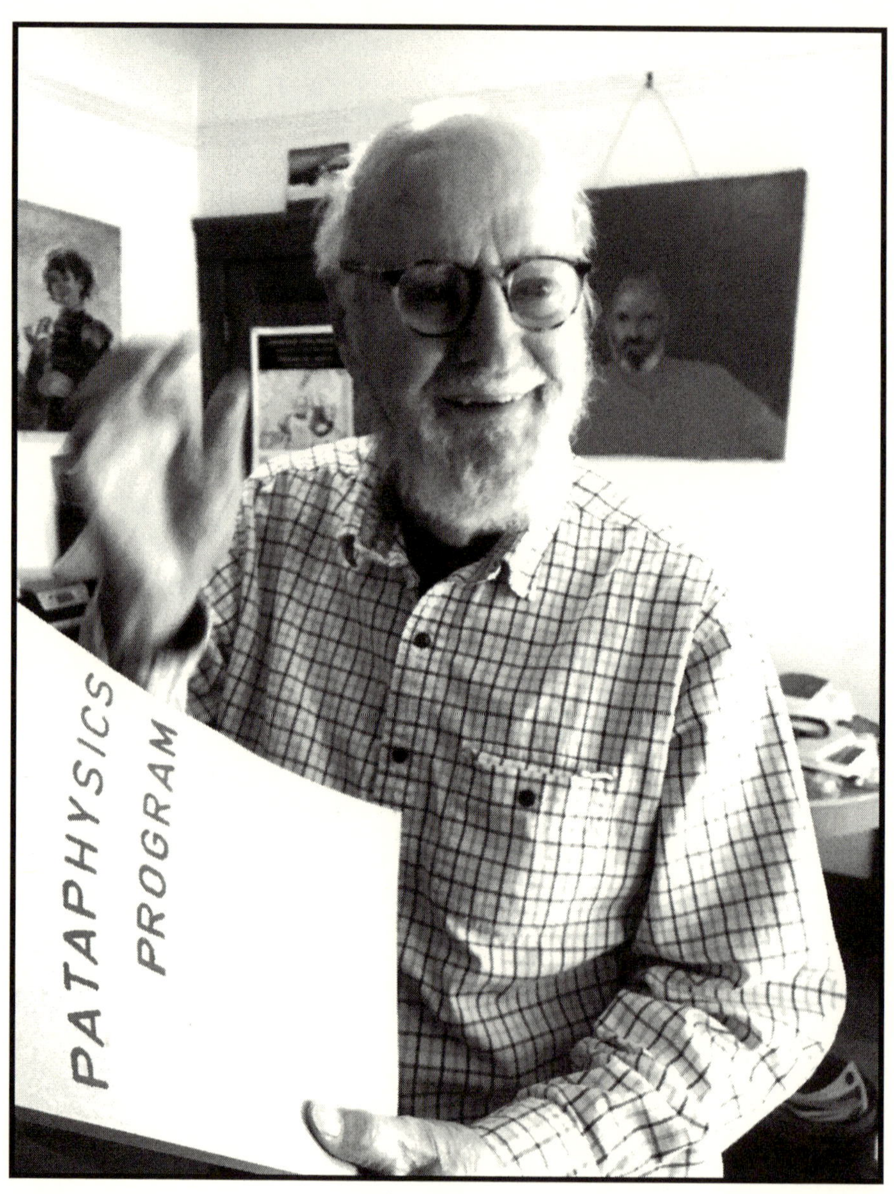

Lawrence in his Apartment II **D.S. Black**
San Francisco, October 12, 2016

Pataphysics: "the virtual or imaginary nature of things as glimpsed by the heightened vision of poetry or science or love can be seized and lived as real" from *Exploits & Opinions of Doctor Faustroll, Pataphysician,* Alfred Jarry (Fasquelle, 1911).

4

Tales

all thought subsumed
in one great thought
(utopian vision!)

"At Sea"—Ferlinghetti

Anecdotes, Musings, and Messages of Gratitude

40 Contributors

Lawrence Ferlinghetti founded City Lights. He gave us his *A Coney Island of the Mind* and he published *Howl*. For these three acts alone he will be forever part of the American Poetry Book. –Indran Amirthanayagam, "Manifesto," "Lawrence Unfurling"

I first read Ferlinghetti in high school, and he has strongly influenced my body of work. "Reading Ferlinghetti During the Pandemic" is a pantoum-cento based on lines from many poems in *A Coney Island of the Mind* and *Open Eye, Open Heart*. The poem borrows Ferlinghetti's words to describe my experience of the pandemic. –Sandra Anfang, "Reading Ferlinghetti during the Pandemic"

Ferlinghetti has been an influence in my life since my childhood. He was one of my mother's favorites, and it was she who introduced me to poetry as a reader and later as a creator. Ferlinghetti has been present in my university studies, in my political and poetic manifestations, in my romantic life, and in my times of solitude. That is a complete poet—breakfast, lunch, and dinner. Ferlinghetti's poetry changed my life, it gave me that spark of creating with freedom, without traditional linguistic ties, that vibration of struggle with what happens every day, the inspiration of the everyday transformed into a revolutionary act, because poetry is Revolution. Your magic library is here, dear Lawrence, with your ideals, with your smile plastered on the walls, helping us to understand how to solve problems with poems. –Adrian Arias, "Home," "Poetic Archetypes," *A million in one*

As Lawrence Ferlinghetti approached his 100th birthday, the inspiration for this book was born. It just appeared one day, a flash of bird-wing in my mind, which settled in to nest. I proposed it to Bobby Coleman, and since Lawrence had contributed poems to two previous Jambu Press titles and praised the outcomes, he happily agreed. When I first moved to San Francisco in 1991 as a young poet with a typewriter (and very little else), I lived on the Chinatown/Nob Hill border. I could easily walk down Jackson Street to North Beach, where I'd steal about almost on tiptoe, hoping to get a glimpse into some imagined, all-embracing poetry scene . . . but it never happened. Not yet acclimated to an urban scene, admittedly I was too shy at the time to read at any neighborhood open mics, which in the early '90s also seemed fewer than now. The only place where I felt wrapped in welcoming arms was the Poetry Room at City Lights Bookstore. What a visionary, nurturing, expansive space Lawrence gifted to the world—and that's just one of the many stars in his cosmic constellation. –Virginia Barrett, "Two Women with Bags," "Naked Lines," *We're All in the Same Boat*

To the extent my work is engaged with the struggle for social justice, I acknowledge the influence of Lawrence Ferlinghetti. My earliest encounter with him was at Naropa's Jack Kerouac School of Disembodied Poetics in 1982, where he proudly asserted his emulation of the French tradition of *littérature engagée* in contrast to many of his American peers, who were content to sup at the trough of academic sinecures, grants from foundations or government agencies, and other compromises to their independence. –D.S. Black, "For Lawrence," *Lawrence in his Apartment I* and *II*

By 2013 I had cultivated a hearty harvest of friends in common with Lawrence Ferlinghetti, but had never met the man himself. The North Beach poetry scene I knew was severe and tempestuous (sometimes a little zany). I rode in with some wild-eyed poets to City Lights, where its 60th anniversary was afoot. In a rare move, Lawrence Ferlinghetti held a meet-and-greet in an alcove upstairs which was ordinarily closed to the public. Guitar hoisted on my back, I entered the quaint office. A group of people zestfully awaited the entry of Mr. Ferlinghetti. The energy was high. I felt the urge to play some revolutionary-themed songs. I serenaded the room until a lady came out and requested I stop playing, in order to create a more tranquil environment. I was a shade crestfallen Ferlinghetti wouldn't hear my music. It was an evanescent wait before Lawrence Ferlinghetti came into the room and its occupants queued up. When my turn came it was challenging because I wasn't verbally prepared to speak with him. We took a photograph together and I asked him if he was going to submit to the next Revolutionary Poets Brigade book. He replied, "Send me an email." –Jim Byron, "Portrait of the Wind"

Before *Pictures of the Gone World* I had never seen a chapbook, and without the inspiration of Ferlinghetti's work I might not have become a poet. "About 7 (Reconfigured)" is an experimental poem, taking Ferlinghetti's poem "Yes" (#7 in that manuscript) and reordering the words and thus the meaning but, I think, retaining the sensibility of Ferlinghetti and his socio-political use of metaphor. – Susana H. Case, "About 7 (Reconfigured)," "Workdays"

A Coney Island of the Mind was part of campus life, a kind of poetic, liberation theology for aspiring poets and other activists. Before comrades at Kent State were gunned down 100 miles away, I remember *Coney Island* lying on a coffee table as we protested the US invasion into Cambodia. 1970. A decade after *Coney Island* was written. Being liberated meant reading a poet who understood the consciousness our middle class upbringings had tried to quash. Ferlinghetti was (may still be) part of my own personal freedom to write. The dream of City Lights, flowers in the barrels of guns, never ends. The amusement park, eternal. The fare is poetry. On pages defying mortality, of Love. –antoinette nora claypoole, "a grief ago"

In 1970, I was living in the basement apartment in the Ferlinghetti's giant red Victorian on Wisconsin Street atop Potrero Hill in San Francisco. Some construction was occurring—and thus, the dumpster in front. I asked Lawrence to put on a sombrero I found in his house and to climb into the dumpster with Homer. He brought along a book titled *Dogs* so he could read to Homer! – Margo Davis, *Lawrence Ferlinghetti Reading to his Dog, Homer, in a Dumpster, Potrero Hill, 1970*

We all owe so much to Lawrence, for his poems since the Fifties, the bookstore and City Lights publishing with all they've brought to the world. May his great work continue with writing and painting both. Keep on trucking Lawrence, long may you run! –Frank Donnola, "North Beach Meander"

I suppose I first encountered the "San Francisco Scene" in the 1957 issue of the *Evergreen Review*. From there it was an easy jump to *A Coney Island of the Mind*. For a time, San Francisco was the glamor center of poetry, and at the very center of the "San Francisco Scene" was City Lights Books. Ferlinghetti's poems had enormous charm and immediacy. Here was a Modernist—a descendant of Pound and Eliot—whose work was immediately understandable, or at any rate seemed to be. If it was not "difficult," as Pound and Eliot were, it was nonetheless immensely enjoyable! –Jack Foley, "Words for Ferling"

People always associate Ferlinghetti with San Francisco, but he was a native New Yorker (Yonkers), and very much enjoyed coming back this way on visits, which was not often. I took these photos on just such a visit, in 1981. Lawrence was usually far more relaxed in New York than in North Beach, where there were always people approaching him for one thing or another. The photo with Carl Solomon (a City Lights author) was taken at a book party at Mickey Ruskin's bar, One University Place. Lawrence is mugging for the camera. In later years Lawrence avoided Manhattan but enjoyed staying with me in my house in Woodstock, NY, and visiting with Ed and Miriam Sanders. Often we would take a cruise on the Hudson River, and Lawrence would reminisce about camping on the river as a Boy Scout. Around 1997 we spent a few days house-hunting along the Hudson, but he decided against it at the last moment. I think the fantasy was good enough for him at that point. –Raymond Foye, *Lawrence Ferlinghetti: visit to New York City, 1981*, photo series (pp. 148–149)

I wish that laundry day was as erotically charged as Mr. Ferlinghetti describes in "Away Above a Harborful" and I want to thank him for making it so in my mind. –Ashley Pryor Geiger, *Oh lovely mammal*

In 1958, stationed at Treasure Island waiting for discharge from the Navy, I first visited City Lights and bought a copy of *A Coney Island of the Mind* that I carried with me throughout my university years and from which I taught throughout my career as professor of Creative Writing and Literature. Now, as Berkeley, California's first Poet Laureate, it was from that same copy that I read at the Koret Auditorium, San Francisco Public Library on March 17, 2019—to celebrate Lawrence Ferlinghetti's 100th year—"Constantly Risking Absurdity" (a poem that I taught in all of my Introduction to Poetry and American literature courses). –Rafael Jesús González, "En el circo del alma / In the Circus of the Soul"

During the Columbia University riots shortly after my father's death and an injury that canceled my tryout for the Steelers, I was shown a picture of Lawrence wearing, like my father on Sundays, a Stetson and boots. I was inspired. Lawrence was the first living poet I read. 51 years later, I realize that every political, spiritual, and even social experience was somewhat or greatly influenced by him. His work—his life—has given me the permission to play. He is a gift that cannot and will not stop giving, and for this gift I have been, am, and will be, forever grateful. –Jeffrey Grossman, "The Poet," "Pop Hat"

Lawrence Ferlinghetti inspires me by his love and understanding of San Francisco (which he has named "an island in the mind"), his poetics fusing a metrical regularity with a freedom of spirit, his longevity, his radical compassion, and his ability to reach out to a wider audience than almost any English-speaking contemporary poet. –Geoffrey Heptonstall, "An Island in the Mind"

Some years ago I came across a recording of Lawrence Ferlinghetti reading "Moscow in the Wilderness, Segovia in the Snow" and was struck by its beauty, rhythm, and wit. The ease of his words and the vivid images of music flowing into and out of people's lives stayed with me. When I was asked to write a poem about the Sacred Grounds Cafe in 2016, I wanted a title with double-imagery. The black bus of Ferlinghetti's Moscow (*down dark straight night roads*) turned into the #21 Hayes bus in San Francisco. My reward was a free meal on the house. –Clara Hsu, "Poets from the Cold, Sacred Grounds in the Light"

Lawrence Ferlinghetti has shown me, through his poetry and through his life, that maybe, with enough time, you can accomplish everything. The ordinary is sacred; humanity and humor honed home help poems. And what would North Beach (and San Francisco and the world) have been like all these years without City Lights and Lawrence Ferlinghetti? –Richard Ivanhoe, "Ferlinghetti Free Association"

I gathered some archival momentos—from relevant to honoring/engaging Lawrence's words, participation, inspiration, leadership in art activism, general wit & wisdom, etc.—that have generated from mutual projects or shared passions. He is a force, of nature and liberation, with steadfast hospitality to others. In his big garden of life, here are a few petals, evidence of his largesse and cosmic/ comic connections. –Annice Jacoby, *Divine*, *City of Poets*, *Undercover*

I first met Lawrence Ferlinghetti in Berkeley in 1993 at an evening with Allen Ginsberg. He was jovial, encouraging, and eager to have me visit him upstairs at City Lights. I was just twenty-two, on my path toward my future at SF State to study and practice theater and write. That year I read *A Coney Island of the Mind* for the first time. A poem had never excited me more. The rhythm, the honesty, the strength in the words, and the line breaks were transcendent. I had found a new level of poem. And the first time I walked upstairs at City Lights and saw Lawrence sitting there—I felt that same excitement all over again. Of course, I thanked him for writing *A Coney Island of the Mind* and he sort of shrugged and said something like—"long time ago—what are you writing?" I stared—dumbfounded and said—"Some really bad poems." He laughed and replied, "Well—keep writing and they'll probably get better." Thank you for all the encouragement, Lawrence. –c.l. kuckenbaker, "-Ferlinforus-"

I found *A Coney Island of the Mind* once when browsing my high school library shelf. It was a revelation that stood apart from any other poems I'd read, and it still rings true today. Ferlinghetti is passion, economy of language, and how to break the line. Recently I picked up *Lunch Poems* by Frank O'Hara at a local bookstore, which I read (not for the first time) during my lunch breaks at work. This time I noticed that Ferlinghetti published that book, which reinforced his sway as a writer and editor. That's when I couldn't help but write my own lunch poem as a tribute. –Richard Landers, "Lunch Poem"

More than a half-century ago, a student teacher accidentally dropped two books on my high school desk: Ginsberg's *HOWL* and Ferlinghetti's *A Coney Island of the Mind.* I was launched. –Ron. Lavalette, "Candy"

City Lights was the main place that I wanted to hang out and did hang out in 1976 when at 17 I first came to San Francisco. I was living on the street, sleeping in Golden Gate Park and panhandling, and would take the N Judah up from the Inner Sunset and then walk up from Market Street to City Lights. My first real apartment in the city later in 1976 was on Pacific & Leavenworth and I would walk down to City Lights all the time and sit in the "Science Fiction Heaven" which at that time was upstairs right above the register, and just read books. Nobody kicked me out. Ferlinghetti was one of the positive spirits that welcomed me into San Francisco and into my life. –John Law, "Atop the Spiral Stair"

My high school art teacher, Donald Fox, gave a copy of *A Coney Island of the Mind* when I was 14. It inspired me further in directions I was already going, such as breaking rules. –Jessica Loos, "Aquatic Park"

I am influenced by Lawrence Ferlinghetti's Zen appreciation of small things like a dog's point of view and a bird disappearing over a horizon. –César Love, "Playland of the Mind"

The poets of the '60s, among them Lawrence Ferlinghetti, were a tremendous inspiration to me as a closeted queer teenager who published my first poems in a neighborhood newspaper when I was 16. Reading and re-reading Ferlinghetti's *A Coney Island of the Mind* affirmed my own questioning of "the establishment," as we called it, a questioning that led to my coming out in 1971. The following year, I became one of three winners of the Temple University Young Poets contest. –Tommi Avicolli Mecca, "For Iris Canada"

I have a deep respect for Ferlinghetti, for his honest eye and deep-rooted integrity, obvious in his poetry. –Karen Melander-Magoon, "Remembering 'In Golden Gate Park that Day . . .'"

I fell in love with the city of the Beat movement. On my first pilgrimage to City Lights, I felt the presence of all the poets who had been there before. I hardly knew a soul on arrival, but City Lights felt like my first San Francisco friend. –Kelliane Parker, "Ode to City Lights," "Boat People"

I was not aware of Ferlinghetti's devotion to painting until years after reading his poetry. When I first saw his paintings, I said to myself, "Ferlinghetti is a painter?" Indeed, he is both poet and painter. His view that the arts are not as striated as we often may think (or as they often are taught), but are unified within an artist, reflects his view of humanity: we are all one. Ferlinghetti, to me, embodies harmony of the arts. –Sara Parrott, "Spotting Ferlinghetti at the Wedding on the Beach"

Ferlinghetti was one of the first poets I read (in my teens then, I'm 66 now) who helped me to see how open one can be in writing a poem. He is like a door, an open door, and he invites us in. –Kenneth Pobo, "A Little Over 6000 Years Ago, "Normal Forest"

Lawrence Ferlinghetti said that "art should be accessible to all people, not just a handful of highly educated intellectuals." That has always guided my own poetry. I give away poems on the street and have on-the-spot readings anywhere, anytime. I have even recited poems upstairs at City Lights to random listeners and stuffed my poems into shelves there. I always wondered if Mr. Ferlinghetti would approve, but I suspect he would. He has an impish side as well. –Jack Prizmich, "Attraction"

I moved to San Francisco from the Midwest in 1963 to attend the San Francisco Art Institute. One of the first things I did was go to City Lights Bookstore—one of the highlights of living here. I started writing poetry in 1965 when the San Francisco Renaissance was in full swing. Seeing Lawrence give a reading of his poetry gave me a whole new idea of what poetry could be about. –Jane Rades, "Coming Home from the Bad Poetry Reading"

I came across Mr. Ferlinghetti's work when I got turned on to the Beats in college. I got a copy of *A Coney Island of the Mind* and loved it. I let a friend borrow it who moved away and I never got it back. I found a copy later at a used bookstore and have been happily married since. –JR Rhine, "Acrostic"

Lawrence Ferlinghetti's light wanders through every poem I've ever composed. I began to admire his verse, his activism, his humor, and his wide-mindedness as a high school student, in Miami, Florida. San Francisco loomed large as a beacon whose call only grew brighter through college, graduate school, and my first real job as a staffer on Capitol Hill. One day in 1997, I walked into the office and gave notice, packed two suitcases, one with clothes and one with books, and bought a ticket to San Francisco. I met Lawrence for the first time over lunch on the day of my first poetry reading. His advice to me was "read more slowly than you think you should and always leave them wanting one more." Now, after dozens and dozens of readings, I never fail to heed this excellent advice. Lawrence is our Homer. May the epic live on. –Tamsin Spencer Smith, "A Principle of Double Reflection"

Ferlinghetti has me in stitches with his jovial and sarcastic sense of humor. –David Volpendesta, "Forbidden Psalm to the Ram at the Pinnacle of the Mountain"

I was born in 1955, the year Allen Ginsberg read "Howl" at Six Gallery in North Beach, and although my poet-trek began in San Francisco, I was not directly influenced by Lawrence Ferlinghetti and the local Beats. I was, however, radicalized (a word I will reclaim) as a teen during the Black Power, Anti-War, American Indian, La Raza, and Feminist movements, which coincided with the cultural force of Ferlinghetti's poetry and publishing that would shape the City where I took my fledgling poet steps. City Lights Books release of Bob Kaufman's writing into the world would touch me first as a poet in the making and again decades later with the publication of *Collected Poems of Bob Kaufman.* In my search for Kaufman, I found part of myself as his work either ignited or rejuvenated a forgotten kind of language in me. –Michael Warr, "What Is Poetry?"

I've loved Lawrence Ferlinghetti since reading *A Coney Island of the Mind* in high school. I think it's his ability to embody contradiction that impresses me. There is humor and outrage, high and low diction, language both wildly figurative and plainspoken. –Cynthia White, "Epiphany"

Meeting Ferlinghetti one morning was a high point in my life as a poet over the last 20-plus years. During many trips before I lived in San Francisco, visiting City Lights was a must. Ferlinghetti founded my favorite independent bookstore, which has the best collection of poetry I know. –Lorraine Walker Williams, "One Morning"

In one of my previous books I published "Poem for Ferlinghetti," which recounts meeting Lawrence. I used to live on Francisco Street as well, by pure coincidence, and I would sometimes frequent a cafe on the end of our street which we called the "Bad Cafe" because of its atrocious coffee. One day I was sitting outside there, and Lawrence sat down next to me and asked if he could have the paper when I was done. I said sure, and watched him take out a manila envelope of what must have been new poems. Eventually I gave him the paper, we chatted, and then I limped off in my cast (I had recently had ankle surgery). I didn't tell him who I was, though we had in the past corresponded. Oddly enough the same thing happened to my best friend, the poet Joshua Beckman, when he was visiting me in the same neighborhood: different cafe, but same thing with the newspaper, same cordial chatting without Joshua telling him who he was, though they too had recently corresponded. Funny life. –Matthew Zapruder, "Poem for Ferlinghetti"

I have the deepest respect for Lawrence Ferlinghetti, whose *A Coney Island of the Mind* blew my mind in the late '60s. Later, post 9/11, The Living Theatre, with whom I acted for 30 years, did a street piece around the RPC circa 2004, in which we quoted a substantial section of "The History of the Airplane." Need I say it struck home? I'm a New Yorker. It struck home. I love that Lawrence Ferlinghetti is an erudite poet who speaks plainly. He is beautifully accessible, yet never simplistic. That in itself is quite a feat, not to mention that his so-called populist approach doesn't compromise the complexity of his work. The fact that he's a fellow anarchist increases my admiration of him as an artist and a mensch. –Joanie HF Zosike, "I Am Also Waiting"

5

In Memoriam

The universe holding its breath
There is a hush in the air
Life pulses everywhere
There is no such thing as death

"A Heap of Broken Images"—Ferlinghetti
(poem title from *The Waste Land*, T. S. Eliot)

My Friend Lawrence Ferlinghetti, 1919-2021

Neeli Cherkovski

Ferlinghetti and I
Would go to the Surf Theater
Way out by Yokohama
He was an aggressive
Driver, his old Volkswagen
Bus had several dents

Driving through the Stockton
Tunnel he'd proclaim,
"We're leaving the Casbah."
And he would chuckle
As he turned left on Van Ness
Leaving North Beach
And City Lights Books

We saw a movie, set in Paris,
The title escapes me, but
Lawrence's excitement
Over the sights, Notre-Dame
In a side view, the Seine
Head-on, Apollinaire's shadow
On Boulevard Saint-Germain

"I should go for a visit," he said,
"Like Henry Miller did."

Two days later we headed
To Bixby Canyon, he said
I could carve my name on
The outhouse wall alongside
Kerouac and Ginsberg

We read from *Leaves
of Grass* that night by
A campfire, "He's like
An older brother,"

Lawrence said of Whitman

A year later
He wrote from
Paris, "I'm bringing you
A new beret, made right
Here."

San Francisco, Paris,
Big Sur, an open
Heart who would
Never grow old,
Who would be an
Ancient bard, who
Would hold a lantern
In the dark

He wrote
The dog
Trots freely
In the street and
Told anyone
Who would listen
The secret meaning
Of Goya's greatest scenes

February 24, 2021

Starting Again Lawrence

Indran Amirthanayagam

I am starting from San Francisco and I am going
to cross the Plains, the wheat and corn fields, then
hop over to New York. At the same time I will
head south to L.A, to San Diego, Tijuana
and then weave through the Mexican states.
I will do this free now of body, not dependent

on buses, trains or airplanes, not even my feet.
Mind breathing Allen said. But over there
in those mountains Gary is still cutting wood
and planting roses, and off in North Beach,
a curlew's cry from City Lights, Jack Hirschman
crafts an arcane. We are industrious, Lawrence,

and in your name. Do not worry about us.
Keep on flying everywhere you wish
unencumbered, and join the cancer survivor
next year with her bionic leg in that X rocket
that will hurtle round the planet. But keep
a discreet eye back here. Infuse us to write

a poem to mark her heroism, and wonder,
and that of all of us living in the coney islands
of waking dreams, that yes we can climb, rise,
soar and come down again laughing wild
in America. We can recover after
remembering our half a million dead

from the virus, each one a rhyme
in the poem we must write now without
you while your spirit still guides our fingers
wherever we say to the blank page, this one's
yours Lawrence, to keep you company
on the journey through now endless worlds.

February 23, 2021

One Red Berry in February

for Lawrence, sleep well poet

Kim Shuck

Somewhere irrespective of brass plaques
Statues
Street names
There are the psychological memorials
The way that some line of poem makes its way into
Another line of poem that may take the idea another step
The mud street becomes
Wooden sidewalk becomes
Concrete sidewalk that is pierced to make space for
A tree that feeds birds in February
Red berries
Red berries in February that don't remember the origin mud or
The wooden sidewalk
But are part of that story
Even so
Somewhere out beyond brass plaques
There is a new generation combing the words
Agreeing or not but
Using the earlier work to build with
To build on
To tear down
Agreeing or not
And somehow
Here
There is a red berry
Here in February
In this poem
That tracks back to a jail cell
And an obscenity trial or maybe
Back to Coney Island but certainly
Through the doors of a bookstore
Where there has been refuge
Mud, wood, concrete, tree, berry, bird and
Whatever comes next

I invented the alphabet
after watching the flight of cranes
who made letters with their legs.
"Autobiography"—Ferlinghetti

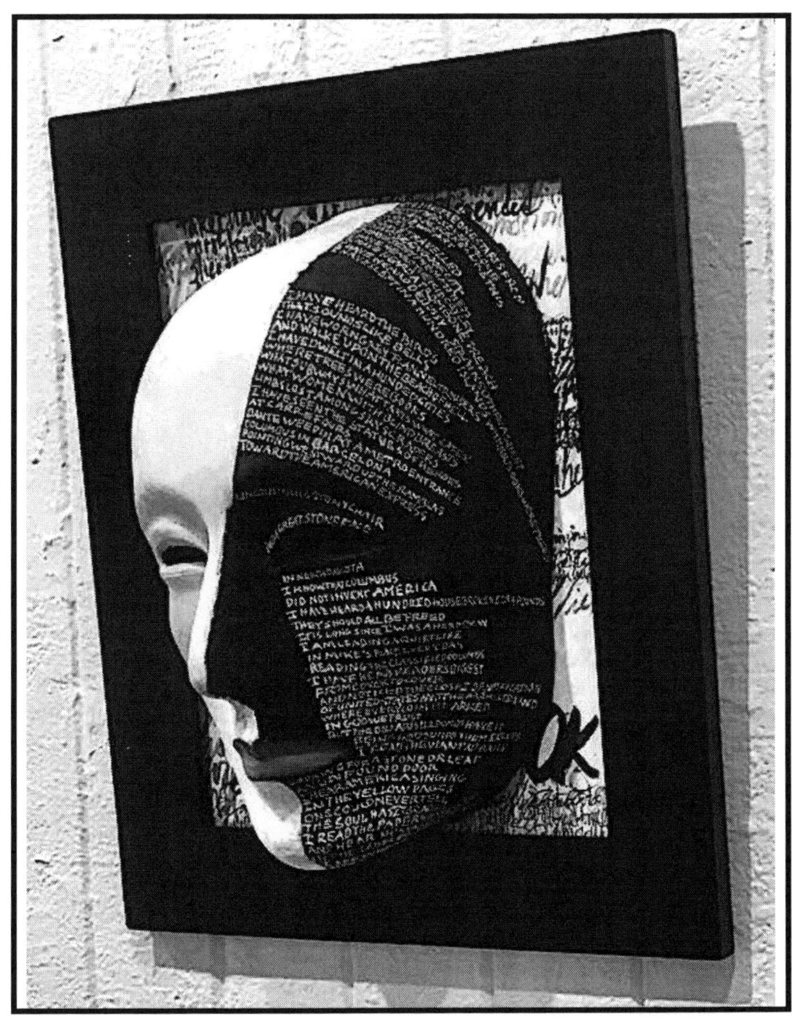

Hear America Singing **Agneta Falk**
acrylic, ink, paint on mask

I made this piece for Lawrence with his poem "Autobiography" written on the side of the mask. Until his passing, it hung on his kitchen wall for years.—A.F.

Lawrence Ferlinghetti Died

Virginia Barrett

after "Allen Ginsberg Dying"—Ferlinghetti

Lawrence Ferlinghetti has died
It's all over the internet
It streams through social media feeds
A great being has died
But his work
won't die
His work is in our island minds
it's in our useful musings
In North Beach
in his own bed
he died
There is no way
to change it
He died the death all life dies
He died the death of a poet,
of an artist, publisher, insurgent extraordinaire
For a century
his bright eyes saw
what the sky sees
what the ocean brings
Blind in his last years
He listened
as humanity heaves under
the weight of greed & need
and left poems for us all
Through the cycles
in the wheel of the world
There is only one Ferlinghetti
The lover Death
has enchanted him
where once he drew
her nakedness
with live open strokes
And stood among the flesh remains
at Nagasaki

a newborn poet-pacifist
He has passed beyond the Golden Gate
His painted vessel out of sight
becoming pure light
He has taken off his Lady Liberty mask
he wears the infinite one
the face of all expression
Lawrence is on the big screen now
playing in the Poetry Room
He climbed the stairs a final time
his office door an OPEN DOOR
His voice is in the air
it fills City Lights everywhere
His breath is in the books
between each line and word
And we hear his new manifesto
the sea weeps in it
the birds sing in it
dissidents no longer hide
It is high tide and the seabirds cry
The water has washed over him
here by the bay
in San Francisco
Where a migrating whale
comes early this year
to weep in the sea
to sing in the sea
A deep sonar song
sonorous waves
sounding through us
Lawrence
                they call
                                Lawrence

The Elegy Arcane
In Memory of Lawrence Ferlinghetti

Jack Hirschman

for Elaine Katzenberger

Addio, Lawrence,
for works well done,
for the poems and
paintings, and the
stands taken for
causes in need of
spreading the word,

you poppalist,
anarchist, common
nest for red birds
and black to fly
into and out of.
You've long been
honored and now

that you belong to
what ages are left
in this holocaustic
pandemic for us all,
we know that your
passing has left the
world angelically

filled with the light
of all you've been:
a fighter but reticent,
a righteous warrior
but gentle of spirit.
That's why the night
of the day you died

I was embraced by
an angel who loved

you so much she
kept you breathing
by way of her own
breathlessness, and
is now transfigured

in the modesty she's
brought to you who
first brought it to her
who can now show
the world the Glory
of the Book we all
know, despite burial

or cremation or any
number of ways your
death is described,
the Book which is
opened at the cover
and into whose depth
you are lain, not to be

buried at all, but to be
read and read and read.

from Ferlinghetti: Poetry Has its Cookies to Give Out

Annice Jacoby

Fortune
    has its cookies to give out
    A Coney Island of the Mind—Ferlinghetti

On February 22, 2021, news of Lawrence Ferlinghetti's death at 101 was not a shock but a hole in the sky. Some people achieve god-like qualities while walking around like mortals made of humble clay. Lawrence was a fixture at City Lights bookshop for decades, so any literary pilgrim would encounter his direct connection to the spirit of place; he was the guardian of the temple he created.

I was teaching a class on artists/activism when the text came with the news. Lawrence could have been the role model for everyone from Ai Weiwei, son of an exiled dissident poet, to Dave Eggers, leading the way for creating *Impossibly Beautiful Spaces for Young Minds on Fire.*

Lawrence animated the role of poet warrior with audacious, original crusades for free thought, free people, and free pursuit of what you damn please. Like Neruda, Ferlinghetti was a bard of imagination in public life. Bravo Lawrence, your words, your painting, your courageous defense of poets and poetry, hospitality to generations of readers and writers. You are instantly missed, and will always be here.

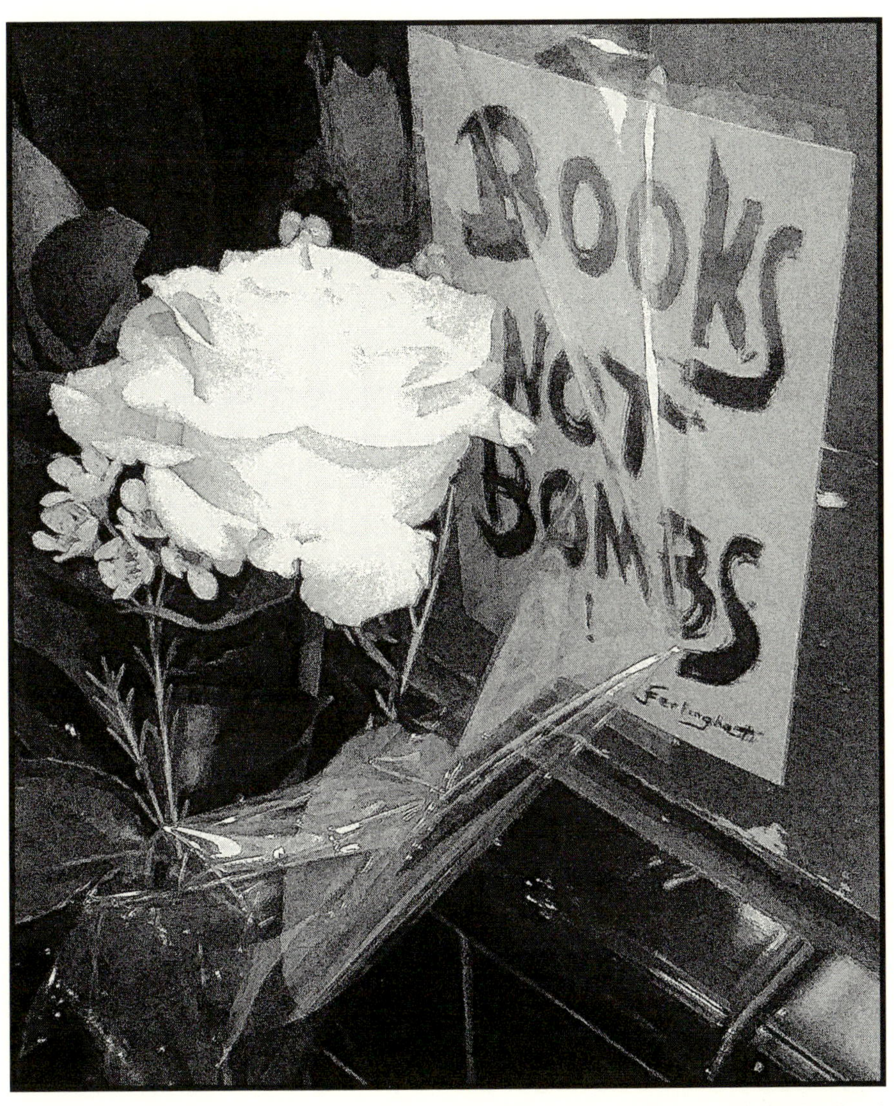

Flowers for Ferlinghetti
City Lights entrance, February 23, 2021

Notes

p. 17 San Francisco's open-mic poetry scene thrives at a wide array of venues, too many to fully list. These include Clarion Performing Arts Center, On the Page/Off the Page, 16th & Mission Mic-less Open Mic, Poem Jam, Word Party, Bird & Beckett, Beat Museum, North Beach First Fridays, Mission Cultural Center for Latino Arts, Poems Under the Dome, libraries, bookstores, schools, festivals, galleries, cafés, bars, clubs, offices, concerts, home gatherings, places of worship, streets, rallies, picket lines, government meetings, and everywhere that poetic voices need to be heard.

p. 26 "I Am Also Waiting" (excerpt, stanzas 1 and 3)—after Ferlinghetti's "I Am Waiting"

p. 31 "to be a poet"—all lines in italics from *Poetry as Insurgent Art*

p. 39 "Candy"—after "The pennycandystore beyond the El . . ." (*A Coney Island of the Mind*, 20)

p. 41 "Lunch Poem"—references *Lunch Poems* by Frank O'Hara, published by Ferlinghetti (City Lights Books, 1964)

p. 44 "Workdays"—references imagery from various poems found in *A Coney Island of the Mind* and *Pictures of the Gone World*

p. 48 "Reading Ferlinghetti during the Pandemic"—based on lines from poems in *A Coney Island of the Mind* and *Open Eye, Open Heart*

p. 60 "The Ferlinghetti School of Poetics"—stanza in italics (*There's a breathless hush on the freeway tonight . . .*) from "Wild Dreams of a New Beginning"

p. 78 "Acrostic"—is partially based on "The world is a beautiful place" (*A Coney Island of the Mind*)

p. 92 "Words for Ferling"—first line in italics from "Endless Life;" lines in parentheses from "Adieu à Charlot (Second Populist Manifesto)"

p. 94 "Spotting Ferlinghetti at the Wedding on the Beach"—a little

Charley Chaplin (charleychaplin in LF's poem) and constantly risking absurdity from "Constantly Risking Absurdity" (*A Coney Island of the Mind*, 15)

p. 101 "Naked Lines"—line *own free world to live in* from "Dog;" *Poets, come out of your closets . . .* from "Populist Manifesto No. 1;" *Away above a harborful* from "A North Beach Scene;" *la vida es sueño real* from "Sueño Real" (originally from Pedro Calderón de la Barca)

p. 111 "Coming Home from the Bad Poetry Reading"—lines in italics (stanza 6) from *Poetry As Insurgent Art*

p. 113 "Transmission"—poet Julie Rogers transcribed an interview with Ferlinghetti by Garrett Caples of City Lights Publishers

p. 119 "a grief ago"—first two lines in italics from "Assassination Raga," *the secret meaning of things* from the LF book title (*The Secret Meaning of Things*, New Directions, 1968) in which that poem appears. The title/phrase *a grief ago* is from "A Grief Ago" by Dylan Thomas in *Twenty-Five Poems* (1936), credited to him by Ferlinghetti in "Assassination Raga." Ferlinghetti first read "Assassination Raga" at San Francisco's Nourse Auditorium on June 8, 1968 for the opening event of a week of "Incredible Poetry" readings at the Nourse and at Glide Memorial Church. The kickoff event occurred on the evening of Robert F. Kennedy's funeral, a day of national mourning following his assassination. Also featured that week were Richard Brautigan, Allen Ginsberg, Joanne Kyger, David Meltzer, John Wieners, Lew Welch, Michael McClure, Gary Snyder, Philip Whalen, and the San Francisco Mime Troupe Gorilla Band; offset lithograph posters for the poetry festival were created by artist Victor Moscoso.

p. 137 *Birthday Crowds, City Lights*—lines from "Matinal"

p. 150 "For Lawrence"—line *through the flames* from *Poetry As Insurgent Art*; *over all the obscene boundaries* from the book title *Over All the Obscene Boundaries*

p. 173 "Lawrence Ferlinghetti Died"—line *becoming pure light* from "At the Golden Gate;" *It is high tide and the seabirds cry* from "Allen Ginsberg Dying"

About the Contributors

silvi alcivar is that girl who talks about death at parties. When she's not making a living as a poet, selling art, and typing on-demand poems, you can find her snuggling bunnies, getting back to teaching in nursing homes, and searching for wild parrots in San Francisco. She's written and sold over 75,000 poems that now live in wallets, on refrigerators, and in an army bunker in Antarctica. She's published in anthologies and journals, performed on stage and radio, and been featured in a documentary film. www.thepoetrystore.net Instagram: @thepoetrystore

Richard H. Alpert is an artist living in Northern California. His work in sculpture, painting, photography, performance, installation, and video has been exhibited worldwide. He received a National Endowment for the Arts Fellowship Grant in Sculpture in 1979. His recent video work has been featured in over 20 U.S. and international film festivals. His video *AVE variation #7* won "Best Editing" in the 2019 Global India International Film Festival / Pune. He has published several art books catalogued by the U.S. Library of Congress and archived at major universities and colleges. www.richardalpertartist.com Instagram: @richalp47

Indran Amirthanayagam writes in English, Spanish, French, Portuguese, and Haitian Creole. His 19 books of poetry include *The Migrant States* (Hanging Loose Press), *Coconuts on Mars*, and *The Elephants of Reckoning* (1994 Paterson Poetry Prize winner). In music, he recorded *Rankont Dout.* He edits the *Beltway Poetry Quarterly*, curates *Ablucionistas*, co-directs Poets & Writers Studio International, and writes a weekly poem for *Haiti en Marche* and *El Acento*. He has received fellowships from the Foundation for Contemporary Arts, the New York Foundation for the Arts, the U.S.-Mexico Fund for Culture, and the MacDowell Colony. He hosts the Poetry Channel at www.youtube.com/user/indranam. www.indranmx.com

Sandra Anfang is a Northern California poet and artist whose work has been published in numerous journals including *Unbroken*, *Rattle*, *New Verse News*, and *Spillway*. Her chapbook *Looking Glass*

Heart was published by Finishing Line Press in 2016. *Road Worrier: Poems of the Inner and Outer Landscape* (Finishing Line Press, 2018) was a Lorien Prize finalist. Her book *Xylem Highway* was published in 2019 by Main Street Rag. Sandra has been nominated for Best Small Fictions and a Pushcart Prize. She is the founder of the monthly series Rivertown Poets and is a California Poet/Teacher in the Schools.

Dominic Angerame has directed more than 35 films, honored by awards from film festivals around the world. His work has also received retrospectives from the Museum of Modern Art in New York as part of their landmark series *Cineprobe*. Angerame has lectured, judged, and presented at many international festivals, museums, and film institutions, and has taught at the San Francisco Art Institute, Stanford University, the School of the Art Institute of Chicago, and elsewhere. Serving as Executive Director of Canyon Cinema from 1980–2012, guiding one of the few surviving distributors of avant-garde cinema, and as a film historian, he has come to be regarded as a major contributor to the field of experimental filmmaking and film culture. www.cinemod.net

Adrian Arias is a prize-winning poet, multidisciplinary performer, visual artist, curator, cultural promoter, and arts educator. Born in Peru, he has lived and worked in the San Francisco Bay Area since 2000, publishing books in Spanish in Peru and in English in California. Co-founder of MAPP and the creator of *Illusion Show*, Adrian won the best poem award at Struga Poetry Evenings in Macedonia in 2009 and is the winner of several major poetry awards in his home country of Peru. www.adrianarias.com

Lynne Barnes was born in the Southern state of Georgia, moved to New York City in 1968 with a front row ticket to *Hair*, then migrated to San Francisco in 1969. She was part of a commune that thrived for twenty years in the Haight-Ashbury, and is a retired psych nurse and librarian. Her poetry memoir *Falling into Flowers* (Blue Light Press, 2017) was the 2017 Rainbow Award winner for Best Gay and Lesbian Poetry, a finalist for the 2018 Eric Hoffer Book Award, and received Honorable Mention in the "Gay" and "Poetry" categories of the 2018 San Francisco Book Festival.

Virginia Barrett (*Light on the Walls of Life* book concept and lead designer) is a poet, writer, artist, and educator. Her six books of poetry include *Between Looking* (Finishing Line Press, 2019) and *Crossing Haight—San Francisco poems* (Jambu Press, 2018). She is the editor of two anthologies of contemporary San Francisco poetry including *OCCUPY SF—poems from the movement* (Jambu Press, 2012). She has twice received writing residency grants from the Helene Wurlitzer Foundation of Taos, New Mexico. She most recently taught "International Poetry / Visual Poetry" in the MFA in Writing program at the University of San Francisco. www.virginiabarrett.com

D.S. Black came to poetry in the osmosis of exile and assimilation. His first encounter with an avant-garde was with the Chicago Surrealist Group after moving from Canada to the U.S. in 1978. At Allen Ginsberg's invitation, he went to Naropa in 1982 to workshop with the surviving cadre of Jack Kerouac's friends and admirers. Since moving to California in 1983, his connection with these writers, artists, and poets has deepened. His dream academy has been getting to know the Beats and their fellow-travelers and literary descendants. After 26 years in San Francisco's Mission District, he now lives in Berkeley, California.

Bob Booker is a longtime contributor to the San Francisco Bay Area poetry scene, co-editor of *Ambush Review*, and Event Coordinator at the Beat Museum in San Francisco's North Beach. He also presently conducts a poetry workshop for seniors in Oakland, California.

Jim Byron is a musician and poet who has released hundreds of original songs. His lyrics and poems have been published in several anthologies since joining the North Beach poetry community in San Francisco in 2010.

Susana H. Case is the author of seven books of poetry, most recently *Dead Shark on the N Train* (Broadstone Books, 2020), winner of a Pinnacle Book Award for Best Poetry Book and a NYC Big Book Award Distinguished Favorite. She is also the author of five chapbooks. Her first collection *The Scottish Café* (Slapering Hol Press, 2002, 2015) has been published in a bilingual English-Polish edition, *Kawiarnia Szkocka* (Opole University Press, 2010). Her works have also been translated into Spanish, Italian, and Portuguese. Case is a Professor and Program Coordinator at the New York Institute of Technology in New York City. www.susanahcase.com

Neeli Cherkovski was born in Los Angeles and attended Los Angeles State College (now Cal State Los Angeles). His many books of poetry include *Animal* (1996), *Leaning Against Time* (2005), *From the Canyon Outward* (2009), and *The Crow and I* (2015). He is the coeditor of *Anthology of L.A. Poets* (with Charles Bukowski), *Cross-Strokes: Poetry between Los Angeles and San Francisco* (with Bill Mohr), and *Collected Poems of Bob Kaufman* (with Raymond Foye and Tate Swindell). Cherkovski also wrote biographies of Lawrence Ferlinghetti and Charles Bukoswki, as well as the critical memoir *Whitman's Wild Children* (1988). He has lived in San Francisco since 1974.

Jerry Cimino founded The Beat Museum in 2003 and currently serves as its Executive Director. Their website is kerouac.com

antoinette nora claypoole landed like a lightning bug into rugged landscapes of change—the way life, connected to Earth, becomes Real. A classic hippie exodus from the East Coast to the West became her pathway into writing, poetry, and many years inside the American Indian Movement (AIM). Seen in a dream while living in Taos, New Mexico, she began the renegade literary press Wild Embers. Awarded an Oregon Literary Arts honor for her current decade-long effort to collect and publish the lost stories of Louise Bryant (1885–1936), she continues to collaborate with dreams. www.louisebryantbook.blogspot.com www.wildembers.com

Bobby Coleman is a poet and the managing editor of Jambu Press in San Francisco. He is a graduate of Columbia and Stanford. jambupress.com studiosaraswati.com/bobby-coleman

Paola Corso is a literary activist, photographer, and author of six books of poetry and fiction all set in her native Pittsburgh, where her Italian immigrant family worked in the steel mills. Corso's latest books are *The Laundress Catches Her Breath* (winner of the Tillie Olsen Award in Creative Writing), *Once I Was Told the Air Was Not for*

Breathing (winner of the Triangle Fire Memorial Association Award), and *Vertical Bridges: Poems and Photographs of City Steps* (Six Gallery Press, 2020). She is the co-founder and a resident artist of Steppin Stanzas, a poetry and art project celebrating city steps, as well as a member of the Ferlinghetti Girls with poets Phyllis Capello and Gabriella Belfiglio, a Brooklyn, New York performance art project celebrating Ferlinghetti's poetry. www.paolacorso.com

Soheyl Dahi is a poet, painter, and publisher of Sore Dove Press in San Francisco. He has published numerous limited edition broadsides and boxed editions of Lawrence Ferlinghetti's artworks through the years. Dahi's own books of poetry are published by Bottle of Smoke Press in New York.

Margo Davis is a photographer and teacher whose work has been published in many publications. She specializes in black and white fine art portraiture. Her photographs are in several major collections including the Bibliotheque National in Paris, Brooklyn Museum, New York City, and Cantor Arts Center, Stanford, California. www.margodavisphoto.com

Lou Dematteis is a photographer and filmmaker covering issues of social, political, and environmental importance around the globe. His photos of San Francisco Lowriders taken in 1979-80 are part of the permanent collection of SFMOMA. His book *Crude Reflections / Cruda Realidad: Oil, Ruin and Resistance in the Amazon Rainforest* (City Lights Publishers, 2008) documents the damaging effects of Chevron's oil exploitation and resulting environmental pollution in Ecuador. His latest film, *The Other Barrio*, is a noir feature about gentrification, corruption, the clash of cultures, and the pursuit of justice, set in San Francisco's Mission District. www.loudematteis.com

Frank Donnola is a poet, San Francisco tour guide, raconteur, and bon vivant, amusing the muse in dilapidated shoes for over 50 years. Poet-vocalist with Tony Vaughan in the '70s art-band Palace Monkeys, his work has been published in *Quasar*, *Lewt*, *Noe Valley Voice*, *Haight Ashbury Literary Journal*, and inside several matchbook covers, ever-devoted to poetry in all its splendid and splintered forms.

Agneta Falk is a Swedish-born poet/painter and member of the World Poetry Movement (Medellin, Colombia) and the Revolutionary Poets Brigade of San Francisco. Her poems have been translated into Italian, Chinese, Spanish, and French. She won the Casa della Poesia Regina Coppola Prize in Italy in 2018.

Jack Foley is a poet and literary critic living in the San Francisco Bay Area. His poetry books include *Letters/Lights—Words for Adelle*; *Gershwin*, *Exiles*, *Adrift* (nominated for a Northern California Book Reviewers Award), *Greatest Hits 1974–2003,* and *Ash on an Old Man's Sleeve*. His books of criticism include the companion volumes *O Powerful Western Star* (winner of the Artists Embassy Literary/Cultural Award 1998–2000), *Foley's Books: California Rebels, Beats, and Radicals,* and *The Dancer and the Dance: A Book of Distinctions.* www.jack-adellefoley.com

Raymond Foye has worked as a literary editor with City Lights, New Directions, and Black Sparrow Press, and as Director of Exhibitions and Publications at Gagosian Gallery. He co-edited and co-published Hanuman Books (Chennai, India and New York, NY) with Francesco Clemente. He received an American Book Award from the Before Columbus Foundation for co-editing *The Collected Poems of Bob Kaufman* (City Lights Publishers, 2020). He is presently co-editing *The Golden Dot: Last Poems 1980–2000* by Gregory Corso (New Directions) and is a Consulting Editor at the *Brooklyn Rail*. www.raymondfoye.info www.brooklynrail.org/contributor/raymond-foye

Ashley Pryor Geiger is an interdisciplinary artist and scholar who lives and works in Toledo, Ohio. Drawing on her extensive research and teaching in the humanities, her visual work uses digital collage and the manipulation of old photographic processes like calotypes, ambrotypes, tintypes, and daguerreotypes to create a bridge between the past and the present—especially as it relates to those who have been forgotten, overlooked, or underrepresented in history. Her work has appeared in numerous print and online journals. Instagram: @ashcat7077

Joan Gelfand is the author of three poetry collections and an award-winning chapbook of short fiction. Her reviews, stories, essays, and poetry have appeared in national and international literary journals and magazines. Joan has taught for California Poets in the Schools, Poetry Out Loud, and currently for The Writing Salon. Her poem "The Ferlinghetti School of Poetics" was made into a short film by Dana Walden, which won Best Poetry Film at the World Film Festival in Los Angeles and has been shown at over 20 international film festivals. *Extreme* (Blue Light Press, 2020), her debut novel, takes place in a Silicon Valley gaming startup. www.joangelfand.com

Matt Gonzalez is a native of McAllen, Texas and received his BA from Columbia College in New York City. He has published two verse collections: *The Violet Suitcase* (San Francisco: Lew Editions, 2011) and *Beauty Will Be Convulsive* (San Francisco: FMSBW, 2021).

Rafael Jesús González is a Professor Emeritus of Literature and Creative Writing, born and raised biculturally and bilingually near the El Paso, Texas / Cd. Juárez, Chihuahua border. He taught at several universities before settling at Laney College in Oakland, California where he founded their Department of Mexican and Latin-American Studies. He was Poet-in-Residence at the Oakland Museum of California and the Oakland Public Library in 1996. González has been nominated four times for a Pushcart Prize, received honors from the National Council of Teachers of English in 2003, and was granted a Lifetime Achievement Award by the City of Berkeley in 2015 for his writing, art, teaching, and social activism. He was named Berkeley, California's first Poet Laureate in 2017. rjgonzalez.blogspot.com

Jeffrey Grossman was born in Pittsburgh and raised in Punxsutawney, Pennsylvania. He majored in American Studies at Rutgers University and received an MFA from Columbia University. He edited the poetry anthology *Beatitude 33: Silver Anniversary* and is the author of *Wampum*, *Grasping the Sparrow's Tail*, and the forthcoming *Amethyst.* His work has appeared in the *Morning Breeze*, *Beatitude*, *Big Hammer*, *North Coast Review*, *American Poetry*, *Temporary Culture*, and other magazines.

Geoffrey Heptonstall is the author of the novel *Heaven's Invention* (Black Wolf, 2016) and two poetry collections, *The Rites*

of Paradise (Cyberwit, 2020) and *Sappho's Moon* (Cyberwit, 2020). He has also written a number of performed and/or published plays. Heptonstall's recent short fiction has appeared in *Pennsylvania Literary Journal* and in *Scarlet Leaf Review*. His essays and reviews have appeared regularly in *Global Dispatches*, *Litro*, and *The London Magazine*. He lives and works in Cambridge, England.

Juan Felipe Herrera is a son of farmworkers and lives in Fresno with his wife, poet Margarita Robles. For the last fifty years he has dedicated his life to poetry, community, art, and teaching. In the last ten years he has served as California Poet Laureate and as U.S. Poet Laureate. His various awards include a National Book Critics Circle Award, Guggenheim Fellowship, *L.A. Times* Robert Kirsch Award, Latino Hall of Fame Award, Pushcart Prize, and a UCLA Gold Medal. He's written over 30 books in various genres, including his recent book *Every Day We Get More Illegal* (City Lights Publishers, 2020). He has lived in San Francisco on-and-off since the '50s–'80s and been a fan of City Lights Bookstore ever since he was a teenager in bellbottoms.

Jack Hirschman was a beloved Poet Laureate Emeritus of San Francisco (2006–2009), a poet/painter, and a translator of poets in nine languages. His *Selected Poems* were published in China in 2018. The fourth volume of his collected poems, *The Arcanes (4th Edition),* was published in 2021 by Multimedia Edizioni of Salerno, Italy.

Anthony Holdsworth is a San Francisco-based painter who works onsite on the streets, primarily in oil on canvas, exploring the environments and landscapes that make up daily life. He aims to transcribe locations as he experiences them—over the course of many days—seeking to translate the essence of the world around us and to shed new light on the relationships between people and the places they inhabit. Holdsworth began painting while working for the Uffizi Gallery in Florence after the disastrous flood of 1966, and continues to travel and paint in Italy. He has exhibited his works in galleries and museums throughout California and beyond. www.anthonyholdsworth.com

Clara Hsu is a Chinese American poet born in Hong Kong. She is a mother, piano teacher, traveler, actor, translator, poet, playwright, purveyor of Clarion Music Center (1982–2005), and Executive Director of Clarion Performing Arts Center (2016–present). Sheltering-in-place during the coronavirus pandemic gave Clara the opportunity to compose music and turn her attention to videography. She wrote and directed a series of comedic skits under the title *Move Over, Corona* and the children's play *The Piano, a Play-Movie*, selected by the 2021 Children's Film Festival Seattle. Clara continues to work with students and gives Chinese poetry classes to seniors in low-income housing by phone. www.clarahsu.com www.theclarionsf.org

Richard Ivanhoe is a Haight-Ashbury neighbor, poet, and activist. You might find him hosting an open mic, at a peace vigil, a neighborhood meeting, or at the Haight-Ashbury Street Fair. He appreciates that in the Haight-Ashbury and in much of San Francisco, writers don't need much imagination—drama, comedy, tragedy are almost always on display. About "Ferlinghetti Free Association" he writes, "I gave a copy (an earlier version) to someone behind the counter at City Lights in 2007. I'm glad somebody else has read it."

Annice Jacoby is a writer and artist. She has created large-scale public artwork including *City of Poets* (with Lisa Citron); *Fort Point Project*, an opening performance at the United Nations Hague Appeal for Peace; the *Oakland Projects* (with Suzanne Lacy and Chris Johnson) addressing youth voices; and helped launch *Watershed* and the environmental campaign *River of Words* (with Robert Hass and *Poetry Flash*). She wrote *Street Art San Francisco: Mission Muralismo* (Abrams, 2009). Annice was Director of Performing Arts at UC Santa Cruz, Director of Public Relations at SFMOMA, and curator of a street art series at the deYoung Museum. PBS has featured her most recent project *Undercover* (organized with Hospitality House), rallying solutions for the humanitarian crisis of homelessness. www.annicejacoby.com

Stella Klar is a poet, collage artist, and photographer originally from Bad Ischl, Austria. She has lived in San Francisco for over twenty-five years and works in a shelter for homeless women and children.

Christopher (c.l.) Kuckenbaker is a writer/actor/director/creator and a resident of San Francisco. He is fortunate to work with EXIT Theatre, Shotgun Players, iO Theater, Redmoon Theater, and Strawdog Theatre. He wanders the streets of San Francisco listening and speaking to the people making San Francisco jump joyful.

Richard Landers was born in the U.S. and grew up in Brazil in the cities of Rio de Janeiro and Belém. His poems have appeared in *Descant*, *Euphony*, *Paterson Literary Review*, *Tampa Review*, and *Roots and Flowers: Poets and Poems on Family* (Henry Holt, 2001). He lives in New York City.

Ron. Lavalette is a widely-published writer living on the Canadian border in Vermont's Northeast Kingdom, land of the fur-bearing lake trout and the bilingual stop sign. His debut chapbook is *Fallen Away* (Finishing Line Press, 2018). His poems and short prose have appeared in journals, reviews, and anthologies, ranging alphabetically from *Able Muse* and the *Anthology of New England Poets* through the *World Haiku Review*. eggsovertokyo.blogspot.com rlavalette.wordpress.com

John Law is the author of a volume of short stories *The Space Between* (Furnace Press, 2008) and co-author of *Tales of the San Francisco Cacophony Society* (Last Gasp, 2013). A member of the SF Suicide Club and the Cacophony Society, Law is co-founder of the Burning Man Festival and the Billboard Liberation Front. A partner and "Special Projects" coordinator for culture blog *Laughing Squid*, Law has also crewed and created props for Survival Research Labs and received his colors as a roustabout for SF Cyclecide Bike Rodeo. Law lives on Russian Hill and has a 15 year old son, Sebastian James.

Brandon Loberg works at the Beat Museum in San Francisco. He writes, "The Beat Museum was founded to preserve the legacy of the Beat Generation and its adjacents, and to perpetuate the values they stood for—tolerance, inclusiveness, and the courage to live your own truth. Lawrence Ferlinghetti, in his life and his work, is fundamental to that movement, and an ongoing source of inspiration for generations well into the future."

Jessica Loos is a poet and event organizer who lives in North Beach. She also does collage, plays tambourine, loves to dance, and is a member of The Living Theatre.

César Love is a Latinx poet who lives in San Francisco, California. He is the author of two books of poetry, *While Bees Sleep* (CC. Marimbo, 2012) and *Birthright* (23rd Street Press, 2016). Love is also the author of *Baseball: An Astrological Sightline* (23rd Street Press, 2019), a book that demonstrates the astrological significance of baseball. He is an editor of the *Haight Ashbury Literary Journal.*

devorah major was born and raised in California and served as San Francisco's third Poet Laureate (2002–2006). Her bilingual sixth book of poetry *with open arms* was released in Italy by Multimedia Edizione in 2019; her seventh book of poetry *califia's daughter* was released in 2020 and is an Aquarius Press / Willow Books Editors Choice awardee. She is a poet, novelist, short story writer, essayist, and performance artist who performs her work nationally and internationally with and without musicians. She has been a participant in international poetry festivals in Italy, Belgium, Bosnia, Jamaica, and Venezuela, and performed her poetry in France, the Bahamas and Germany. www.devorahmajor.com

John Paul Marcelo began painting amidst the urban decay of Chicago streets, only imagining the natural grandeur in faraway lands. After graduating from college having studied graphic design and advertising, he made the sudden choice to reject modern technological mediums, paint exclusively en plein air, and migrate to the majestic California coastline. Residing in the Bay Area, he has blended social and environmental awareness into his work. Although he's content to paint idyllic scenes like Big Sur and Marin, he's documented places like post-Katrina New Orleans, California's wildfires, and the Union Carbide factory in Bhopal, India. www.jpmarcelo.com

Tommi Avicolli Mecca is a southern Italian queer poet, activist, and performer whose poetry has appeared in newspapers, magazines, and anthologies since the late '60s. His latest theater piece *the old brown jacket* has been performed at Monday Marsh and at Solo Sundays at Stage Werx. Originally from working-class

South Philadelphia, he now lives in San Francisco and has worked for the Housing Rights Committee, a tenants rights organization.

Karen Melander-Magoon has always written, whether songs or poems, and has performed in four of the musical shows she's written—about Georgia O'Keeffe, Clara Barton (founder of the American Red Cross), Lillie Langtry, and the women of Greek mythology. Her books of poetry are *A Year of Anguish, A Time for Miracles* (Bowker, 2020) and *The Earth Turns* (Bowker, 2020). When she was seventeen, *Seventeen Magazine* published her poem, "Dawn." She has degrees in music from Indiana University, counseling/ education from Boston University, and a doctorate in ministry from the Graduate Theological Union. She loves birds and people, especially her children and grandsons. She is a member of the Revolutionary Poets Brigade. www.karenmm.com

Janice Mirikitani was San Francisco's beloved second Poet Laureate (following Lawrence Ferlinghetti). She authored five books of poetry including *Out of the Dust* (University of Hawaii Press, 2015). She edited nine landmark anthologies which provide platforms for writers of color, women, youth, and children. With her parents, she was incarcerated in an Arkansas concentration camp with the mass internment of Japanese Americans during World War II. Mirikitani, and her husband Reverend Cecil Williams co-founded the Glide Foundation, which for the past 50-plus years has achieved worldwide recognition as a groundbreaking organization empowering San Francisco's poor and marginalized communities.

Alejandro Murguía is the sixth San Francisco Poet Laureate Emeritus and a two-time winner of the American Book Award. His most recent book is *Stray Poems* (City Lights Publishers, 2014). He is a Professor of Latina/Latino Studies at San Francisco State University. www.alejandromurguia.org

Ira Nowinski is a photographer whose published and exhibited work includes *No Vacancy: Urban Renewal and the Elderly* (C. Bean Associates, 1979), *Café Society: Photographs and Poetry from San Francisco's North Beach* (with poems by Ferlinghetti, Cherkovski, Ginsberg, Norse, et al., Two Continents Publishing Group, 1978), *A Season at Glyndebourne* (Trafalgar Square Publishing, 1989), *Ira*

Nowinski's San Francisco: Poets, Politics, and Divas (Heyday, 2006), and *In Fitting Memory: the Art and Politics of Holocaust Memorials* (Wayne State University Press, 2018). His photographs are represented in the following public collections: Green Library (Stanford University), Bancroft Library (UC Berkeley), Library of Congress, Bibliothèque nationale de France (Paris), Museum of Modern Art (New York), SFMOMA (San Francisco), and the National Museum of Photography (Bradford, England). www.iranow.com

Kelliane Parker is a queer, Latinx, Bay Area street poet. She fled L.A. for a life of art and poetry. City Lights was her first San Francisco friend. To visit there is to go to church, to convene with the ancestors, and to travel astral planes. Her work has been featured in various anthologies including *Have You Heard Us Yet?* and *Colossus: Home*. She has co-hosted My Word Open Mic in Berkeley, California for the past three years.

Sara Parrott is a poet whose work has appeared in *Michigan Quarterly Review*, *Nine Mile Magazine*, *Stone Canoe*, *Literary Nest*, *Dappled Things*, *Ghost City Review*, and *True Chili*. Several of her haiku have been featured on posters created by the Syracuse Poster Project, including a commemorative poster celebrating the fiftieth anniversary of Onondaga Community College in Syracuse, New York. She holds an MA from Binghamton University. Sara's first book of poetry is *Tipping the Water Jar of Heaven* (Nine Mile Art Corp, 2020).

John Perino has been a San Francisco-based photographer since 1974 and has photographed in Russia, parts of Eastern Europe, Cuba, India, and several countries in South America. After forty years of living in San Francisco, John returned to his hometown of Milwaukee, Wisconsin in August 2020. www.focusgallerysf.org johnperino@yahoo.com

Marc Petrie's work has been published in *City Lights Review*, *Pearl*, *California Quarterly*, and other journals, and has been featured on APR's *Writers Almanac*. He is the author of *Poems of Nature and Despair* (Finishing Line Press, 2021), the novel *A Dream Once Dreamed* (Lulu Publishing Services, 2020), and the poetry collections *The Orange Love Spoon* (Laguna Poets Press, 1998) and *Then All Goes Blue*

(Pacific Writers Press, 1997). Marc helped organize the first two Earth Days. An award-winning Santa Ana, California middle school teacher, he lives in Tustin with his wife, son, and two dogs.

Kenneth Pobo has published ten books and twenty-one chapbooks including *Lavender Fire, Lavender Rose*, winner of the 2020 chapbook contest from Brick/House Books, Stonewall Division, and the poetry collection *Uneven Steven* (Assure Press, 2020). His work has appeared in *Amsterdam Review*, *The Fiddlehead*, *Hawaii Review*, *Atlanta Review*, *Nimrod*, *Brittle Star*, and elsewhere. From 1987–2020, Kenneth taught English and Creative Writing at Widener University in Pennsylvania. www.facebook.com/kenneth.pobo www.twitter.com/kenpobo

Karen Poppy is a San Francisco Bay Area writer whose work has been published in numerous literary journals, magazines, and anthologies. Her recent chapbooks include *Every Possible Thing* (Homestead Lighthouse Press, 2020), *Crack Open / Emergency* (Finishing Line Press, 2020) and *our own beautiful brutality* (Finishing Line Press, 2021). An attorney licensed in California and Texas, her far-ranging interests include artisanal soap-making and equestrian pursuits. www.karenpoppy.com

Jack Prizmich is a teacher, filmmaker, tarot-reader, and poet. A longtime Berkeley resident originally from San Pedro, California, Jack's interest in writing began when he published an underground newspaper as a student in the Food for Philosophy Program at the University of California, Santa Barbara. His work has been published in zines and blogs on various platforms, and a collection of his poems is forthcoming from Not Dead Yet Press. He lives with his wife Katy, artist/teacher and muse, in their house "Hozomeen" (named after Jack Kerouac's meditative mountain in *The Dharma Bums*). He has two children and five grandchildren. His favorite expression is "Ah, Life!" jackprizmich@gmail.com www.facebook.com/jprizmich

Jane Rades is from Wisconsin and has lived in San Francisco since 1963. She received a B.A. in Painting from the San Francisco Art Institute and has exhibited at SF Open Studios and other venues. She has published two books of poetry, *Midnight at Mom and*

Dad's (Beatitude Press, 2012) and *Five Decades, A Rosary of Poems* (Beatitude Press, 2008). In 2012 she also published a book on the Tarot, *Two Years in the Tarot: Portrait of the Artist as a Young Fortuneteller,* and she has recently published a Tarot deck, *The 1969 Tarot.* www.janerades.com

JR Rhine is a poet, musician, and educator living in St. Mary's County, Maryland. His cat is named Lugosi, and his newest collection of poems is *Expired Damages* (jrrhinepoetry.bigcartel.com). His 2021 book *Jimmy Loves His Long Hair* is illustrated by Genevieve Lacroix. Twitter: @jarjarrhine; Instagram: @jrrhinepoetry

Julie Rogers has authored several books of poetry including *House of the Unexpected* (Wild Ocean Press, 2012), three recent chapbooks from Omerta Publications—two written with her late husband, Beat poet David Meltzer—and a CD, *Two-Tone Poetry & Jazz.* She teaches creative writing for Litquake and has coached kids, teens, and adults in writing for many years. She is the Founder and Director of TLC (Transitional Life Care), a Buddhist end-of-life education and support program, www.tlcserves.org, and is the author of *Instructions for the Transitional State,* an end-of-life manual. www.julrogers.com

Piero Roccasalvo Rub is an Italian artist and graphic designer who also works in experimental film, video, and theater. He studied at Accademia di Belle Arti di Venezia and Middlesex University Fine Art, London. www.facebook.com/piero.roccasalvorub

Kim Shuck was the seventh Poet Laureate of San Francisco. Shuck is solo author of seven books, and one of them was the seventh in a series. As you can see Kim is a very lucky person and knows it. Shuck's most recent book is *Exile Heart* (That Painted Horse Press, 2020).

Tamsin Spencer Smith is a poet, painter, novelist, and essayist. Her collections of poetry include *Word Cave* (Risk Press, 2018), *Between First and Second Sleep* (FMSBW, 2018), and *Displacement Geology* (FMSBW, 2021). Her verse appears in various anthologies and journals. *XISLE, a novel* was released in late 2020. Her paintings have been widely exhibited in the San Francisco Bay Area. Smith also writes art reviews and catalog essays, including the recent "A Summer Drawing Circle: The Story of Joan Brown's Mary Julia Series" (George Adams Gallery, 2020).

Richard Stone has spent a good part of his life as a custodian pushing envelopes with a broom and filling dumpsters for the U.S. Postal Service. In his spare time, he's an ardent labor, political, and community media activist (APWU union rep, SF Labor Council Delegate, SF Green Party County Council, Zeitgeist Movement, and KPFA's Community Advisory Board). He also sings and recites the songs and poems of Leonard Cohen with the vocal group Conspiracy of Beards.

David Volpendesta is the co-editor with Barbara Paschke of the Central American short story collection *Clamor of Innocence* (City Lights, 1988). He also contributed translations to the Central American poetry collection *Volcán* (City Lights, 1983) edited by Alejandro Murguía and Barbara Paschke. The title for his poetry collection *Forbidden Psalms* (Vagabond, 2021) was suggested by Lawrence Ferlinghetti in conversation. His reviews of Ferlinghetti's work as well as interviews with him have appeared in the *San Francisco Chronicle*, the *San Francisco Examiner*, and *Poetry Flash.*

Michael Warr is a San Francisco poet whose books include *Of Poetry & Protest: From Emmett Till to Trayvon Martin* (W.W. Norton, 2016), *The Armageddon of Funk*, and *We Are All The Black Boy*. He is the recipient of the 2020 Berkeley Lifetime Achievement Award. Other honors include a San Francisco Library Laureate, Creative Work Fund Award, PEN Oakland Josephine Miles Award for Excellence in Literature, Black Caucus of the American Library Association Award, and an NEA Fellowship. He is translated into Chinese by poet Chun Yu in their "Two Languages / One Community" project. https://michaelwarr-creativework.tumblr.com

Cynthia White's poems have appeared in *Massachusetts Review*, *Narrative*, *ZYZZYVA*, *Grist*, and *CALYX*, among others. She was a finalist for both the *New Letters*-Patricia Cleary Miller Award and the *Nimrod*-Pablo Neruda Prize and the winner of the 2018 Julia Darling Memorial Poetry Prize from Kallisto Gaia Press. She lives in Santa Cruz, California.

Lorraine Walker Williams is the author of five books of poetry and the creator of *ArtPoems.org*, an artist / poet collaboration. Twice nominated for the Pushcart Prize, she has read at the Library of Congress and at the San Francisco Legion of Honor. She was awarded Dodge Foundation grants at the Fine Arts Work Center in Provincetown, Massachusetts and honored as Literary Artist of the Year in Fort Myers, Florida. She has also received awards from the National League of American Pen Women and from numerous publications. An online poetry journalist, workshop presenter, and NJ Summer Bard, she organizes and chairs writing groups in New Jersey and Florida. www.lorrainewalkerwilliams.com

Daisy Zamora is the author of numerous poetry books, translations, and collected political essays. She edited the first comprehensive anthology of Nicaraguan women poets published in Latin America. Her latest poetry collection is *La violenta espuma* (Visor Libros, 2017). Her poetry appears in anthologies in thirty languages including the *Oxford Book of Latin American Poetry*. Bilingual collections of her work include *The Violent Foam* (Curbstone Press) and *Riverbed of Memory* (City Lights Publishers). Among her literary awards are the *Mariano Fiallos Gil* National Poetry Prize of Nicaragua and the California Arts Council Fellowship for Poetry. She was featured in Bill Moyers' PBS series *The Language of Life* and in director Jenny Murray's award-winning 2018 documentary film *¡Las Sandinistas!* She currently teaches at San Francisco State University and gives readings and lectures throughout the world.

Mauro Aprile Zanetti is a San Francisco-based polymath, multilingual author, and multimedia storyteller. Born in Sicily and a *cum laude* graduate of the University of Pisa, he was Lawrence Ferlinghetti's personal aide, secretary, and publicist from 2015–21. He has also held prominent posts as a curator, journalist, speechwriter, professor, media strategist, and filmmaker, including collaborations with the Faggin Foundation, the Smithsonian Institution, and others. Currently, he is Chief Evangelist at Cloud4Wi for the humanization of technology and serves as Philanthropy, Arts, and Culture Advisor to the Manetti Shrem Foundation. www.linkedin.com/in/mauroaprilezanetti

Matthew Zapruder is the author most recently of *Father's Day* (Copper Canyon Press, 2019) and *Why Poetry* (Ecco—HarperCollins, 2017). He is Editor-at-Large at Wave Books and teaches in the MFA in Creative Writing Program at Saint Mary's College of California.

Andrena Zawinski is a poet, flash fiction writer, and avid shutterbug. She has been reading Ferlinghetti since sneak-ordering *A Coney Island of the Mind* as a girl from a backpage ad in one of her mother's romance magazines. Imagine her delight when she gave a reading of her work at City Lights Bookstore years later for LaborFest! Her poetry has received awards for lyricism, form, spirituality, and social concern. Her books include *Landings, Something About* (PEN Oakland Josephine Miles Award), and *Traveling in Reflected Light* (Kenneth Patchen Prize). A veteran teacher of writing, Zawinski is also founder of the San Francisco Bay Area Women's Poetry Salon and the Features Editor at PoetryMagazine.com. www.poetrymagazine.com/zawinski

Joanie HF Zosike, *The Writer's Hotel* Sara Patton 2019 Award recipient is the featured poet in *The New Guard*'s BANG! of August/September 2020. She teaches the Pandemic Poetry Workshop at the School for Creative Judaism in New York City. Her work has been published in *11/9: The Fall of American Democracy* and in Silver Birch Press's *Ides: A Collection of Poetry Chapbooks*. Her poems also appear in *Bastille*, *Dissident Voice*, *Heresies*, *Home Planet News*, *The Forward*, *Levure Litteraire*, *MAINTENANT: A Journal of Contemporary Dada Writing and Art*, *Public Illumination Magazine,* and *Syndic*. Author of seven plays and four solo theatre works, she has received an Albee fellowship and a Foundation for Jewish Culture grant. Joanie acted with The Living Theatre for 30 years, directs DADAnewyork, and co-directs Action Racket Theatre.

In memoriam, we also honor the recently departed contributors to this tribute to Lawrence Ferlinghetti, San Francisco's first Poet Laureate: Janice Mirikitani (the city's second Poet Laureate) and Jack Hirschman (the fourth). With Diane di Prima (the fifth), all passed during this book's production and are very deeply missed.

Credits

Some poems in this collection first appeared in other publications:

silvi alcivar, "to be a poet," *Poets 11 Anthology 2010* (Friends of the San Francisco Library)

Virginia Barrett, "Two Women with Bags" *Crossing Haight—San Francisco Poems* (Jambu Press, 2018); "Naked Lines" *Singing My Naked Lines* (Poet Song Press, 2012)

D.S. Black, "For Lawrence," broadside (100 copies)

Paola Corso, "Mute Poets," *Ovunque Siamo: New Italian-American Writing*, Covid-19 Issue 1

Geoffrey Heptonstall, "An Island in the Mind," *Poetry Quarterly*, 2016

Susana H. Case, "Workdays," *BigCityLit*, 2020

Jack Foley, excerpt from"The Splendid Life of the World," *Poetry Flash* and *O Powerful Western Star: Poetry & Art in California* (Pantograph Press, 2000)

Joan Gelfand, "The Ferlinghetti School of Poetics," *Fog and Light: San Francisco through the Eyes of Poets Who Live Here* (Blue Light Press, 2021), *newworldreview.com*, *Marsh Hawk Review*, *Sparring with Beatnik Ghosts*, *Levure Littéraire* (Best Poem), *DuPage Valley Review*, *Poets 11 Anthology 2010* (Friends of the San Francisco Library), *Bay Area Poets Seasonal Review*

Matt Gonzalez, "The Letter and Syllable," broadside (FMSBW, 2020)

Jack Hirschman, "The Ferlinghetti Arcane," (X-Ray Book Co., 2011); "The Elegy Arcane," citylightsbook.tumblr.com, February 25th, 2021

Annice Jacoby, excerpt from "Ferlinghetti: Poetry Has its Cookies to Give Out," annicejacoby.medium.com, February 23rd, 2021

Karen Poppy, "Marina Safeway, San Francisco," *Naugatuck River Review* (11th Annual Narrative Poetry Contest Finalist), *Fog and*

Light: San Francisco through the Eyes of Poets Who Live Here (Blue Light Press, 2021)

Julie Rogers, "Transmission," *Street Warp* (Omerta Publications, 2013)

Kim Shuck, "One Red Berry in February," Poem of the Day (San Francisco Public Library, February 25th, 2021)

Tamsin Spencer Smith, "A Principle of Double Reflection, *Displacement Geology* (FMSBW, 2021)

Matthew Zapruder, "Poem for Ferlinghetti" *Come on All You Ghosts*. Copyright © 2010 by Matthew Zapruder. Reprinted with the permission of The Permissions Company, LLC on behalf of Copper Canyon Press, www.coppercanyonpress.org

Andrena Zawinski, "Anchorless in the Light," *Delmarva Review* 12, 2019; "What Poetry Is," *Found Poetry Review*, 5, 2013

A note on the Playland postcard (p. 19): this mid-1920s view was likely illustrated by San Francisco's Pacific Novelty Co. from an earlier photograph by James Kenneth Piggott and son Harold B. Piggott of J. K. Piggott Co., 86 Third Street. That building still stands. Such images and other novelties like It's-It, an ice cream treat exclusively sold at the amusement park for decades, served to cement the city's reputation as a creative place at the edge of *that 'continent of the spirit' just beyond the tip of my nose . . .*—Ferlinghetti's *Back Roads to Far Places* (New Directions, 1971).

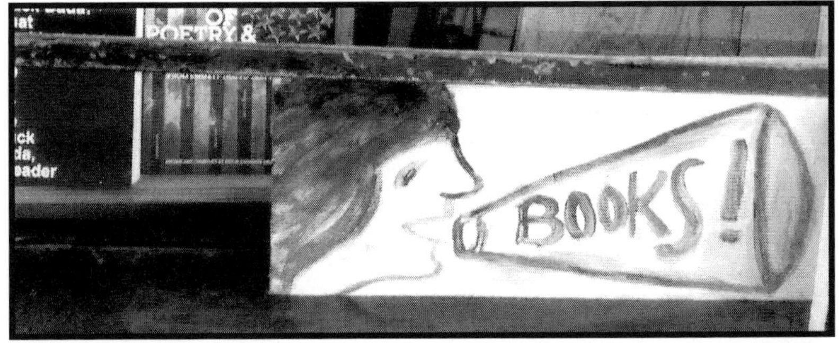

In the Window, City Lights

Poetry is a book of light at night
dispersing clouds of unknowing

What is Poetry?—Ferlinghetti